YOU CAN DRAW MANGA CHIBI CHARACTERS, CRITTERS & SCENES

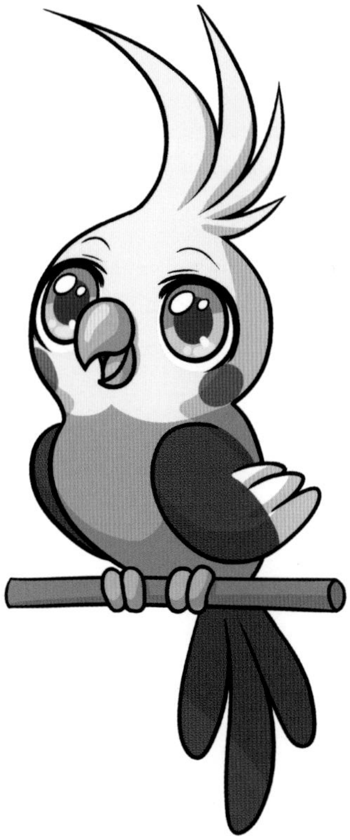

Samantha Whitten & Jeannie Lee

Walter Foster Jr.

Brimming with creative inspiration, how-to projects, and useful information to enrich your everyday life, quarto.com is a favorite destination for those pursuing their interests and passions.

First published in 2020 by Walter Foster Jr., an imprint of The Quarto Group.
100 Cummings Center, Suite 265D, Beverly, MA 01915, USA.
T (978) 282-9590 **F** (978) 283-2742 **www.quarto.com** • **www.walterfoster.com**

Walter Foster Jr. titles are also available at discount for retail, wholesale, promotional, and bulk purchase. For details, contact the Special Sales Manager by email at specialsales@quarto.com or by mail at The Quarto Group, Attn: Special Sales Manager, 100 Cummings Center, Suite 265D, Beverly, MA 01915, USA.

ISBN: 978-1-63322-864-1

Digital edition published in 2020
eISBN: 978-1-63322-865-8

Printed in China
10 9 8 7 6 5 4 3

YOU CAN DRAW
MaNGa
CHIBI
CHaRaCTeRS,
CRiTTeRS & SCeNeS

A step-by-step guide for
learning to draw cute and colorful
manga chibis and critters

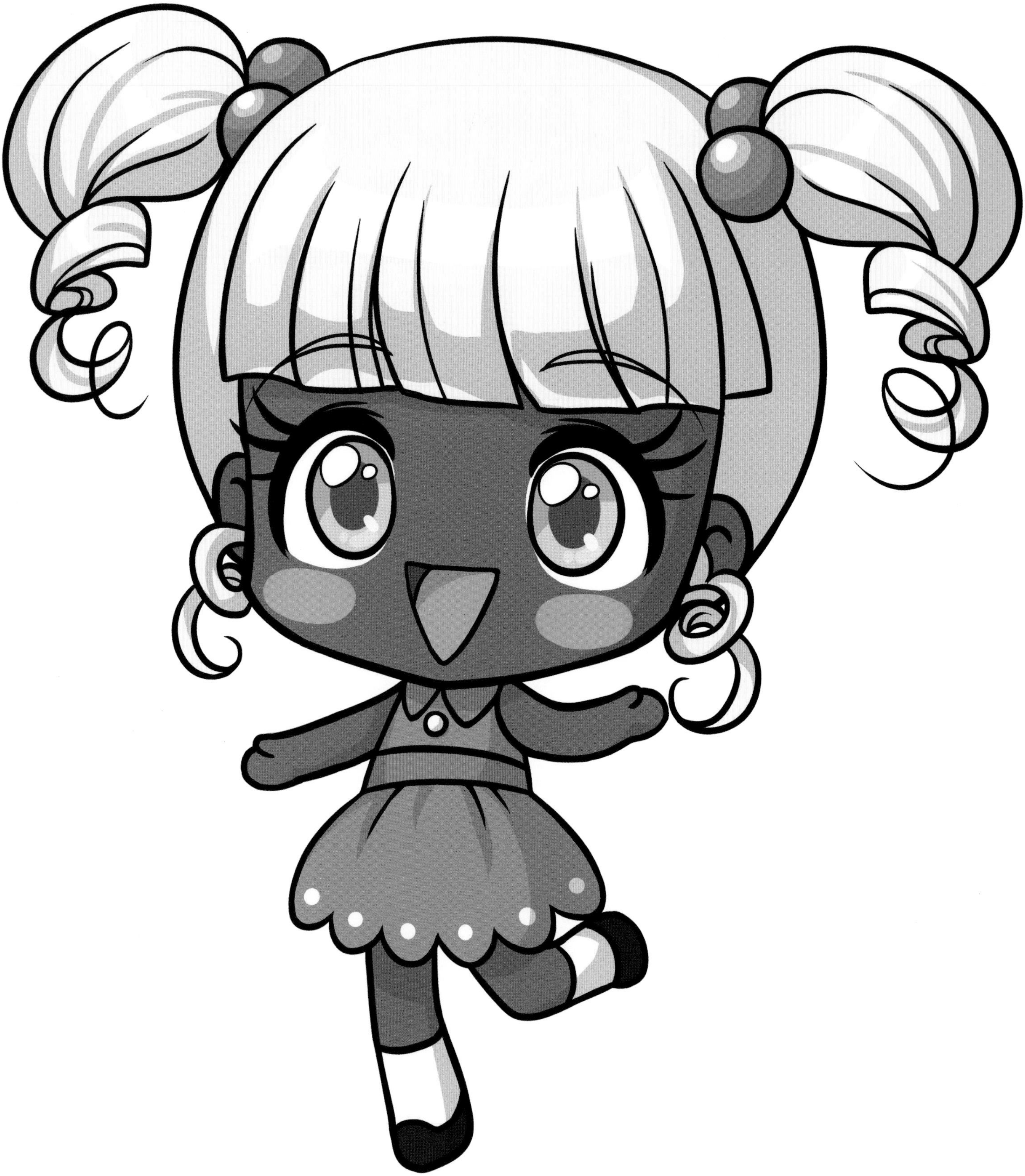

table of contents

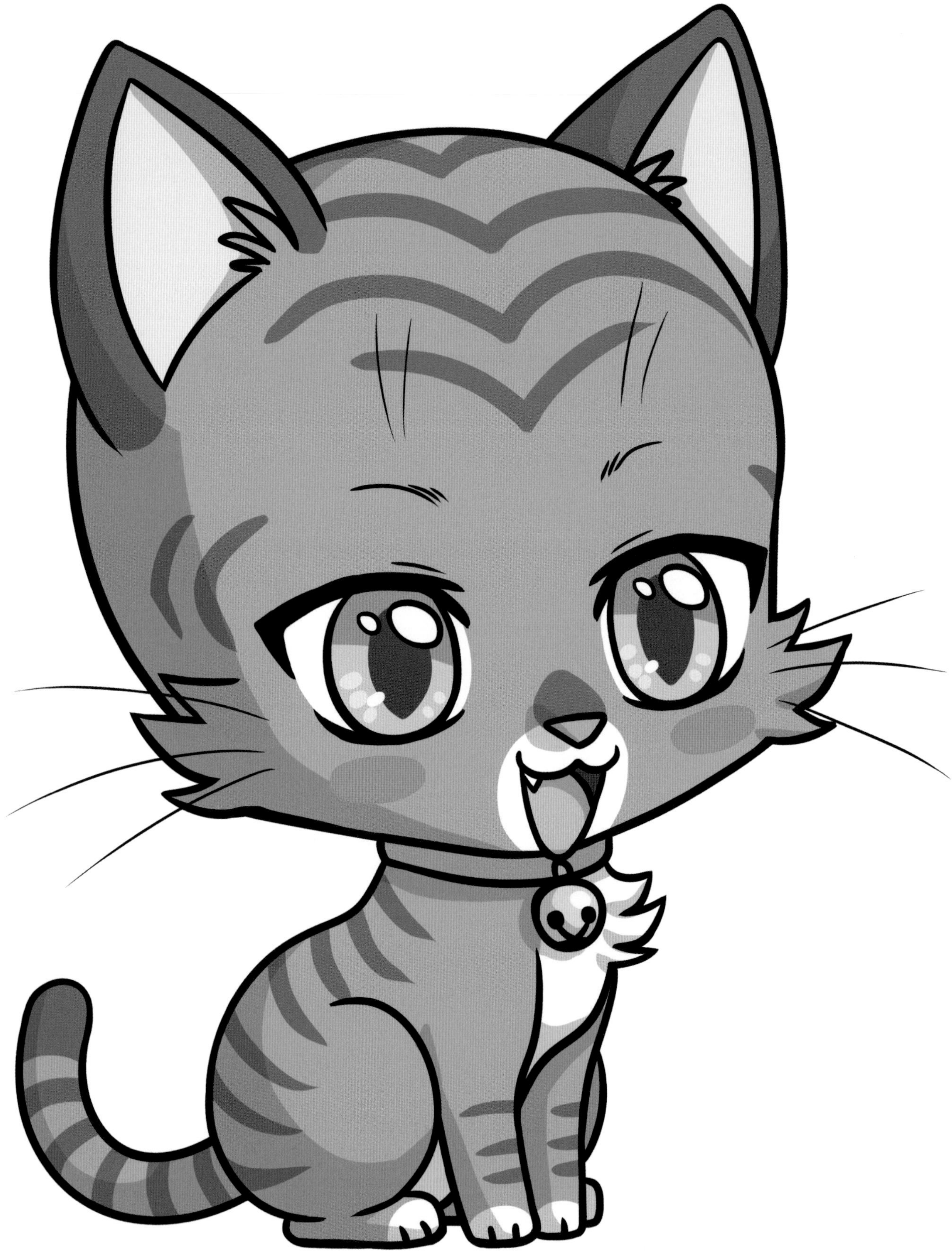

introduction

You know them well—you're reading your favorite manga or watching an anime and suddenly a chibi appears. The word *chibi* (pronounced "chee-bee") means "little" in Japanese. Chibis are supercute caricatures of people or animals that have been shrunken and squashed into funny, childlike creatures with big heads, stubby proportions, and silly expressions. In this book, you'll learn to draw all sorts of chibis. You'll also discover how to "chibify" props, furniture, and other background elements. And because companion critters are a common theme in anime and manga, you'll also learn to transform common animal friends into chibis. So what are you waiting for? A world of adorable chibis awaits! In the name of cuteness, let's dive in and get started!

tools & materials

The artwork in this book was drawn and colored on a computer, but don't worry if you're not set up for that. You can create all of the projects featured in this book with traditional media, such as pencils, colored pencils, pens, crayons, and paints. Below are the supplies you may want to have handy to get started.

▶ **PAPER** Sketchpads and inexpensive printer paper are great for working out your ideas. Tracing paper is useful for tracing figures and creating a clean version of a sketch using a light box. Finally, cardstock is sturdier than thinner printer paper, which makes it ideal for drawing on repeatedly or for heavy-duty artwork.

▼ **BLACK FINE-LINE MARKER** Use a black fine-line marker to tighten your lines and add the finishing touch to your final color artwork.

▼ **ERASERS** A vinyl eraser and a kneaded eraser are both good to have on hand. A vinyl eraser is white and rubbery; it's softer and gentler on paper than a pink eraser. A kneaded eraser is like putty in that you can mold it into shapes to erase small areas. You can also gently "blot" a sketch with a kneaded eraser to lighten the artwork.

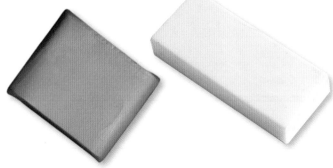

▲ **PENCILS** Pencil lead, or graphite, varies in darkness and hardness. Pencils with a number and an H have harder graphite, which marks paper more lightly. Pencils with a number and a B mean the graphite is softer and looks darker on paper. We recommend H or HB pencils (HB pencils are equivalent to No. 2 pencils) for sketching exercises. In general, use harder pencils (H) for lighter, thinner lines. Use softer pencils (B) for bolder, thicker lines.

► **ART MARKERS** Art markers are perfect for adding bold, vibrant color to your artwork. They are great for shading and laying down large areas of color.

▲ **PENS** Different inks work well for coloring. When buying pens, look for "waterproof" or "archival ink" printed on the side of the pen. Look for pens that release ink consistently for inking line art over sketches.

▲ **COLORED PENCILS** Colored pencils layer over each other easily. They are user-friendly, and some are even erasable!

◄ **PAINTS** Have fun exploring acrylic, watercolor, or good old-fashioned poster paint. Make sure to research what types of paper work well with each paint.

how to use a Light box

As its name suggests, a light box is a compact box with a transparent top and light inside. The light illuminates papers placed on top, allowing dark lines to show through for easy tracing. Simply tape your rough drawing on the surface of the light box. Place a clean sheet of paper over your original sketch and turn the box on. The light illuminates the drawing underneath and will help you accurately trace the lines onto the new sheet of paper. You can also create a similar effect by placing a lamp under a glass table or taping your sketch and drawing paper to a clear glass window and using natural light.

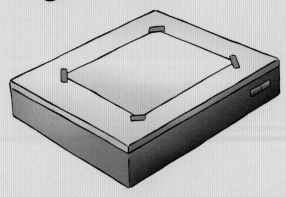

drawing techniques

WARMING UP

Warm up your hand by drawing random lines, scribbles, and squiggles. Familiarize yourself with the different lines that your pencils can create, and experiment with every stroke you can think of, using both a sharp point and a dull point.

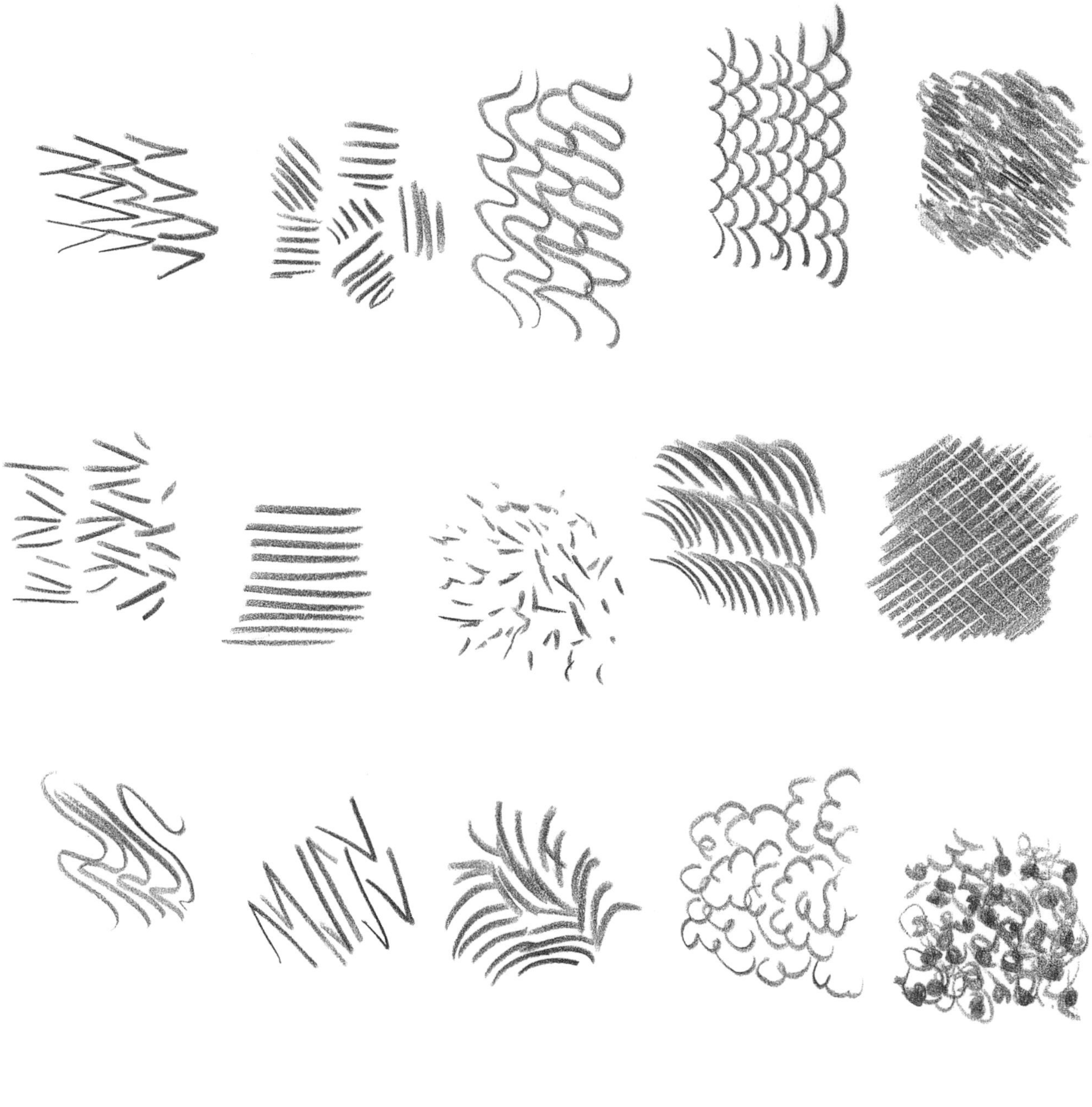

TYPES OF STROKES

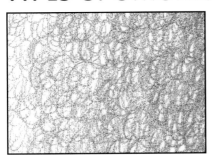

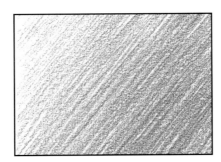

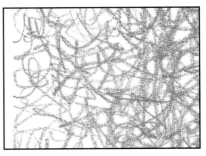

CIRCULAR Move your pencil in a circular motion, either randomly (shown here) or in patterned rows. For denser coverage, overlap the circles. Varying the pressure creates different textures.

LINEAR Move your pencil in the same direction, whether vertically, horizontally, or diagonally. Strokes can be short and choppy or long and even.

SCUMBLING Scribble your pencil in random strokes to create an organic mass. Changing the pressure and the amount of time you linger over the same area can increase or decrease the value of the color.

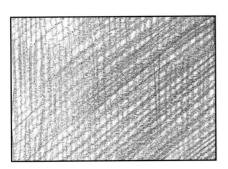

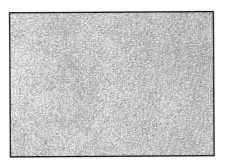

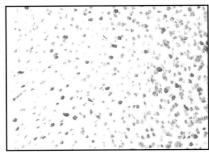

HATCHING Sketch a series of roughly parallel lines. The closer the lines are to each other, the denser and darker the color. Crosshatching involves laying one set of hatched lines over another, but in a different direction.

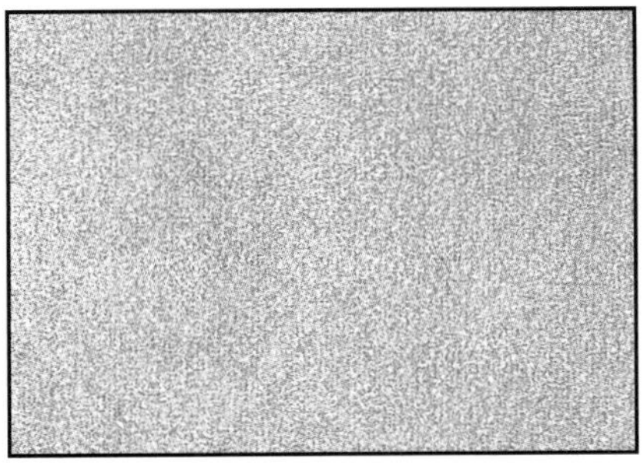

SMOOTH No matter what stroke you use, if you control the pencil, you can produce an even layer of color. You can also blend your strokes so that you can't tell how color was applied.

STIPPLING Sharpen your pencil and apply small dots all over the area. For denser coverage, apply the dots closer together.

COLOR basics

Color can help bring your drawings to life, but first it helps to know a bit about color theory. There are three *primary* colors: red, yellow, and blue. These colors cannot be created by mixing other colors. Mixing two primary colors produces a *secondary* color: orange, green, and purple. Mixing a primary color with a secondary color produces a *tertiary* color: red-orange, red-purple, yellow-orange, yellow-green, blue-green, and blue-purple. Reds, yellows, and oranges are "warm" colors; greens, blues, and purples are "cool" colors. See the color combinations on the next page for more mixing ideas.

THE COLOR WHEEL

A color wheel is useful for understanding relationships between colors. Knowing where each color is located on the color wheel makes it easy to understand how colors relate to and react with one another.

Yellow
Yellow-Green
Yellow-Orange
Green
Orange
Blue-Green
Red-Orange
Blue
Red
Blue-Purple
Red-Purple
Purple

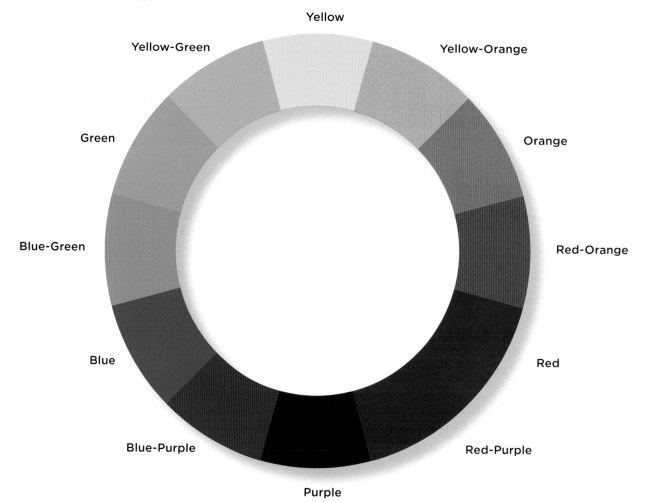

EASY COLOR COMBINATIONS

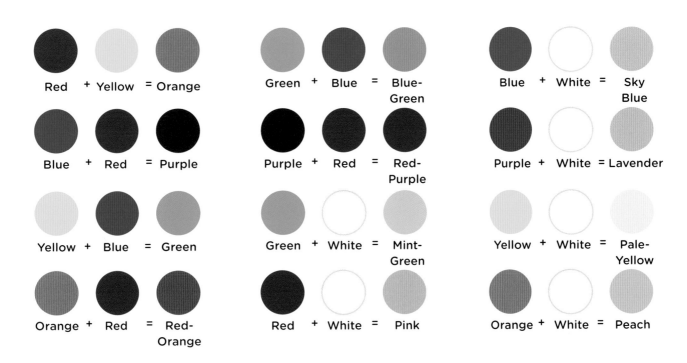

Red + Yellow = Orange

Green + Blue = Blue-Green

Blue + White = Sky Blue

Blue + Red = Purple

Purple + Red = Red-Purple

Purple + White = Lavender

Yellow + Blue = Green

Green + White = Mint-Green

Yellow + White = Pale-Yellow

Orange + Red = Red-Orange

Red + White = Pink

Orange + White = Peach

ADDING COLOR TO YOUR DRAWING

Some artists draw directly on illustration board or watercolor paper and then apply color directly to the original pencil drawing; however, if you are a beginning artist, you might opt to preserve your original pencil drawing by making several photocopies and applying color to a photocopy. This way, you'll always have your original drawing in case you make a mistake or you want to experiment with different colors or mediums.

what makes it a chibi?

The one attribute that sets chibis apart from other anime or manga characters is their proportions. They are squashed and simplified, and their features and sizes are altered to make them look as cute as possible. Common traits include an oversized head, a small body, stubby limbs, and big eyes.

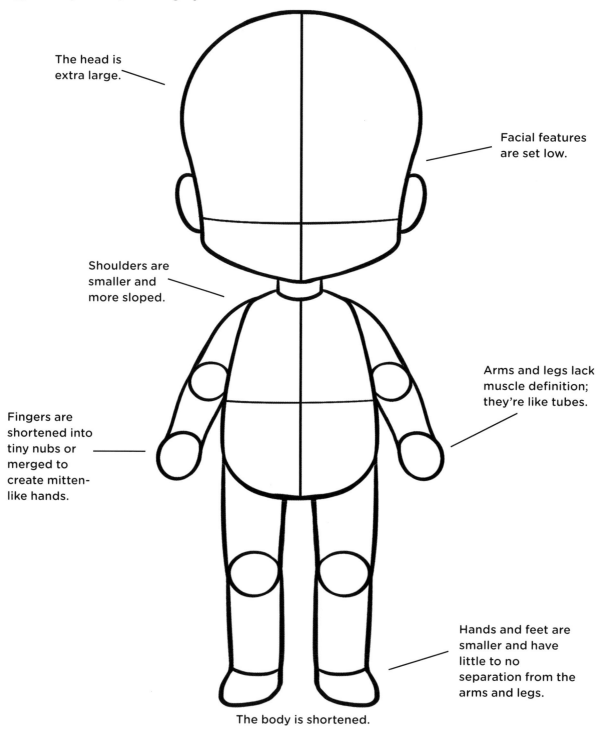

The head is extra large.

Facial features are set low.

Shoulders are smaller and more sloped.

Arms and legs lack muscle definition; they're like tubes.

Fingers are shortened into tiny nubs or merged to create mitten-like hands.

Hands and feet are smaller and have little to no separation from the arms and legs.

The body is shortened.

basic construction

These diagrams illustrate how the proportions of a normal-sized character are different from those of a chibi. A chibi's head is several times larger than a normal head, with lower guidelines for the facial features. Additionally, a chibi's arms and legs are half the typical length. Body parts are chubbier and rounder in chibi form, but this doesn't necessarily mean the character is fatter. Next to a normal figure, a chibi may resemble a child, even if it's not. A chibi character is merely a simplified version of a normal-sized character.

PRACTICE MAKES PERFECT!

Use the templates beginning on page 82 to practice drawing a wide range of chibi characters. You can either scan the templates to your computer and print them out, or photocopy them from the book.

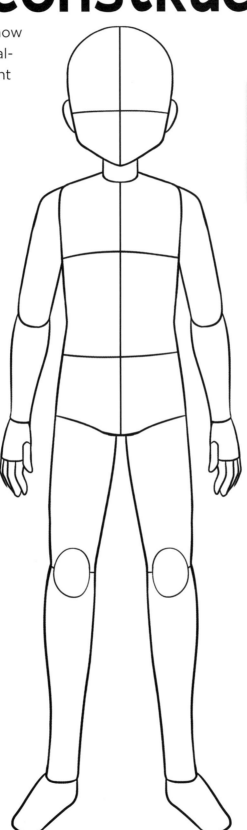

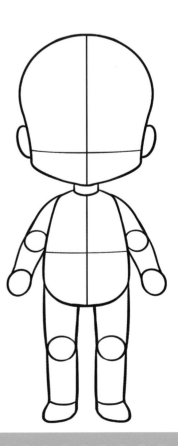

basic chibi face

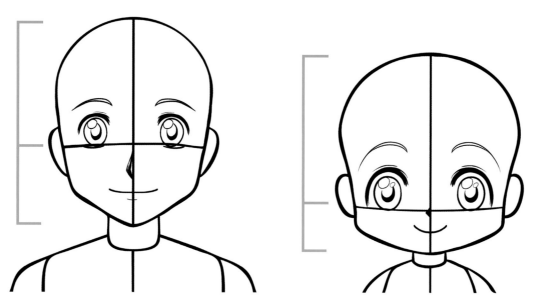

FRONT VIEW

Compared to a normal face, chibi facial features are larger and sit toward the bottom half of the face. The forehead is large, and the eyes are wider and set below the center of the face. Chibi eyebrows arch more dramatically around the shape of the eyes, resulting in a wide-eyed, childlike expression. The chibi nose is a tiny triangle, and the mouth is shorter. Also note the rounder, wider head; flattened chin; and short, thin neck. Use the blue guidelines to measure the differences in proportion and placement between the upper and lower halves of each face.

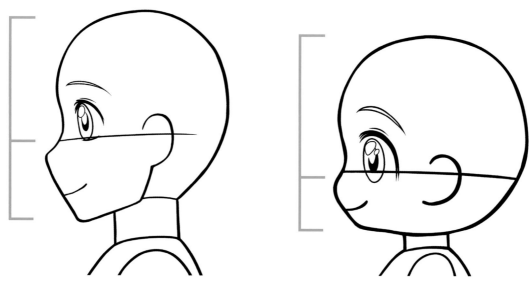

SIDE VIEW

In the side view, also called the profile view, the facial features are still compact and placed lower on the face, resulting in a larger, broader forehead. The jawline and chin are smoothed out and simplified, which makes the chibi character appear shorter and pudgier. The head is more circular, whereas the eye and eyebrow are larger and more pronounced. A small protruding bump indicates the nose, and the mouth and neck are both shorter. You'll also notice the ear doesn't connect to the edge of the jawline.

basic chibi body

Chibis come in all shapes, sizes, and proportions, but the most common body shape is shown below. In this example, the body and legs are approximately the same height, and the head is larger than both! Artists often invent their own measurements and proportions, and you should do the same. If your chibis do start to resemble normal-sized children, tweak the image. Making the head larger is a good first step.

The four most common angles are the front, side (profile), back, and three-quarter views. Note how the shape of the head changes from each angle, and how the arms and legs indicate which direction the character is facing. Even if the angles change, the character still appears to be the same shape, height, and size from all views.

tip

Use basic shapes, including circles, cylinders, and guidelines, to start your drawings. Skipping this step may result in your characters appearing out of proportion.

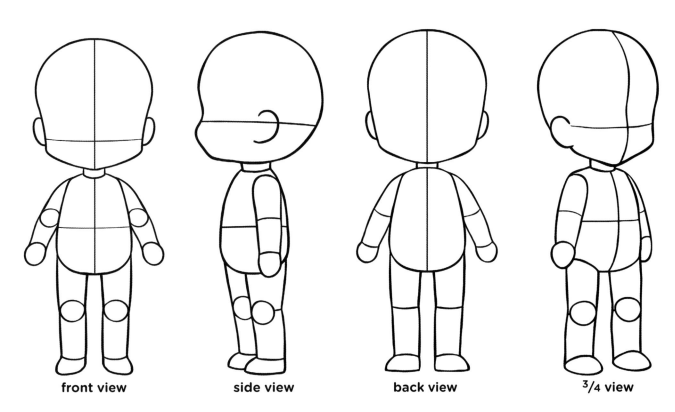

front view   side view   back view   ³/4 view

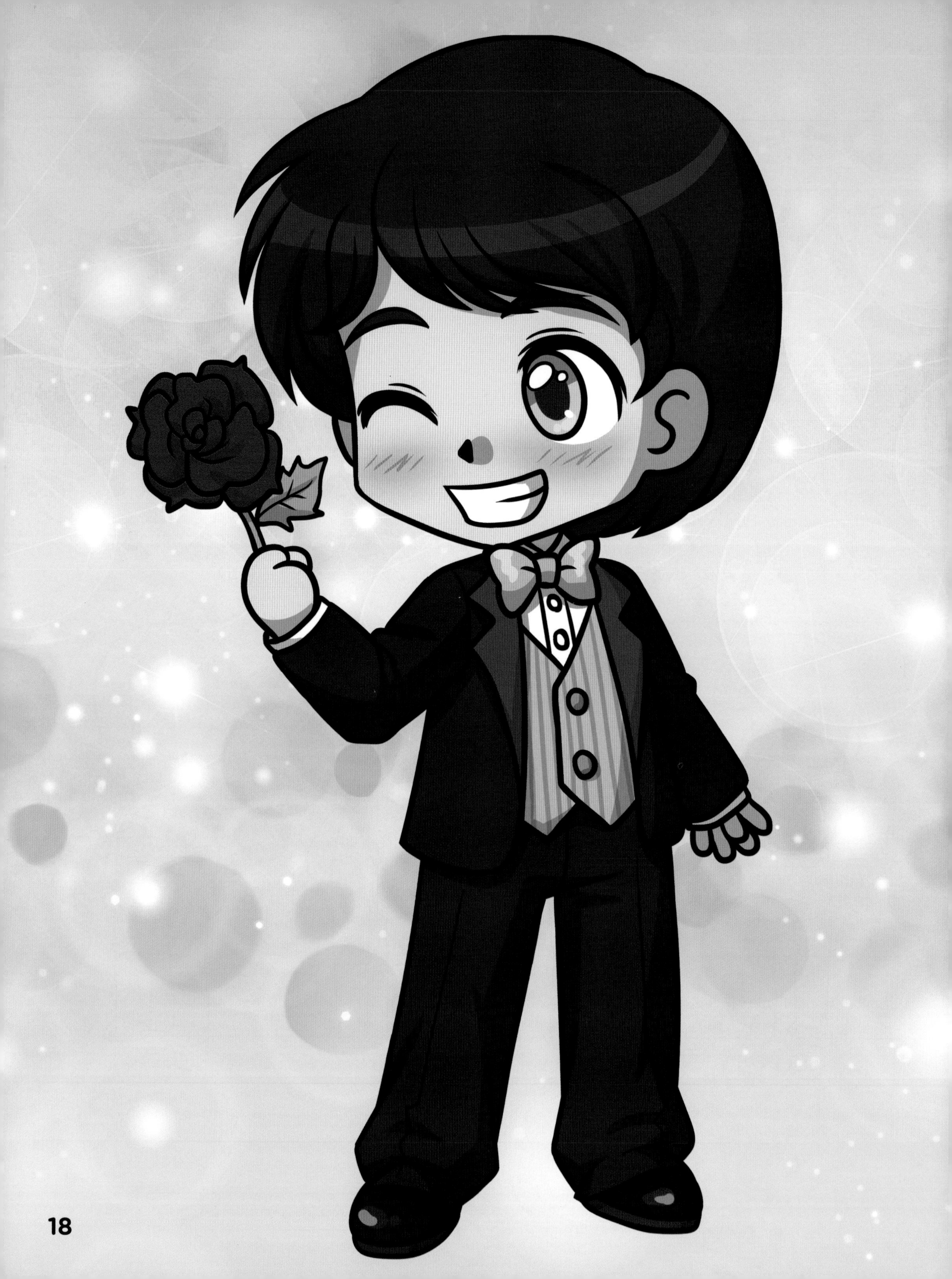

chapter 1
chibi details

chibi eyes

Eyes define a chibi's personality as much as style and pose. And they're particularly important where chibis are concerned because they're often extremely large in proportion to the face. As you review the eyes below, think about what they communicate to the viewer. What might you be able to tell about a chibi's mood just from looking at the eyes?

TRADITIONAL
The eyelids and eyebrows arch upward, and the eyeballs are oval-shaped and clear. Add long lashes or leave them off.

ALMOND-SHAPED
The eyelids have narrow outer edges for a focused look. Add eyelashes or makeup if desired.

DOE
Long eyelashes, white highlights, and a furrowed brow communicate innocence or a shy personality.

SLY
Crafty characters and villains are good candidates for this eye style.

GIRLY
These eyes usually sport makeup, a star-shaped highlight, and lush eyelashes.

CONCAVE
Characters with these eyes are probably solemn, deep thinkers.

HAPPY
The eyes of overjoyed or cheerful characters will close and form curved arcs.

WINKING
This is a popular expression for happy-go-lucky characters with go-getter attitudes.

IRRITATED
Use this expression for frustrated or suspicious characters. Enhance the look by having the eyebrows gather in the center and angle downward.

CLOSED/SLEEPING
With pondering, wishing, or sleeping characters, draw both eyes closed with the eyelashes and arcs of the eyelids pointing downward.

SAD
Add white shiny spots to the insides of the eyes for a "welling up" appearance.

SURPRISED/SHOCKED
Eyelids are large and extend outward in wide, circular shapes, and the irises are small with a lot white space around them.

EXERCISE YOUR CREATIVITY!
Practice making several expressions with your eyes in front of a mirror to become familiar with the different looks they create. Then grab a pencil and paper, and try drawing them!

chibi expressions

Facial expressions convey a character's emotions and mood. Chibi expressions tend to be highly exaggerated, often for comical effect. The combination of an over-the-top expression with a chibi's simplified style results in a wealth of character and feeling. Check out the illustrations on these pages to see how various expressions translate between forms. And always remember that there are plenty of other ways to render each emotion.

HAPPY/CHEERFUL
The arcs of the chibi's eyelids and smile are exaggerated.

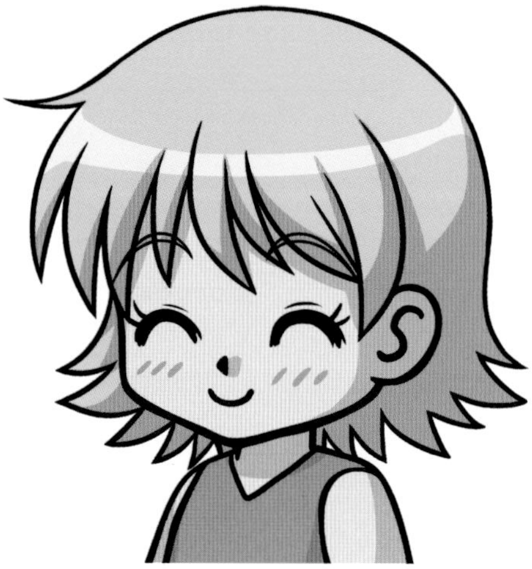

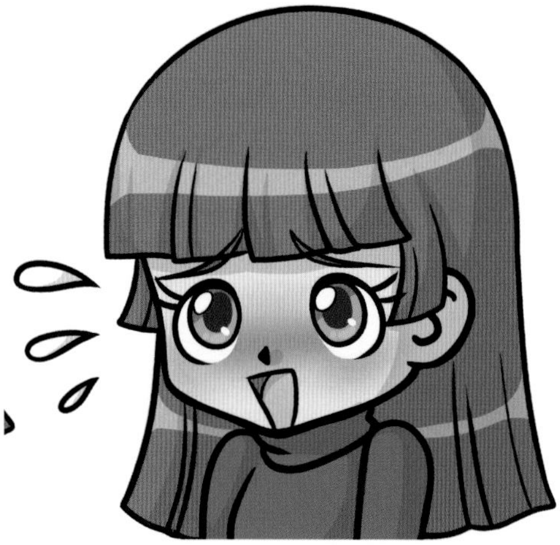

EMBARRASSED/ BASHFUL
A flush covers all of her small face, and sweat drops fly off her.

UPSET/CRYING
Jets of water come from the sides of the chibi's eyes, and her mouth is grossly exaggerated.

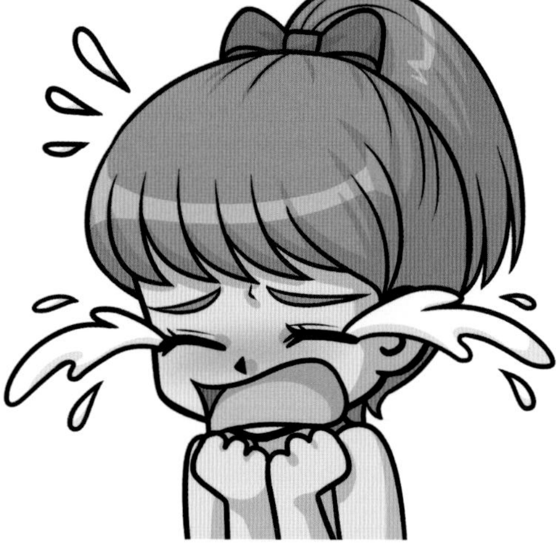

CONFUSED
Question marks bounce off this confused boy's head.

ANGRY
Anger gets more comical in chibi form because the character appears so worked up he could explode.

EXHAUSTED
Even the gust of air is bubble-shaped to look more chibi-like.

SHOCKED
A yellow star-like icon is frequently used to indicate a flash within the mind or to suggest that something is physically jolting.

EXERCISE YOUR CREATIVITY!
Make a list of expressions, including any from this section. Next, sit in front of a mirror with a pencil and paper, and start drawing! If you get stuck, simply make the face you're trying to draw in the mirror and translate it into your drawing—it's a trick even professional artists use.

hairstyles

A hairstyle is important when developing a chibi character because a chibi's shape lacks detail. Some chibi styles are so simplified that the only distinguishing feature between characters is the hair and clothes. Drawing the right hairstyle can enhance a character's look and personality—and there are virtually no limits. Hair can be any length, style, color, or shape.

LONG, STRAIGHT
The key characteristics of this traditional style are its blunt edges and straight bangs. Pair a dark color with this style for a bold statement.

PIGTAILS
There are many ways to draw pigtails and ponytails. This hairstyle is good for cheerful, fun-loving characters.

BRAIDS
This character has symmetrical braids. To draw less complex braids, simply sketch them as outlines, as demonstrated in the sketch at left. Characters who are shy or studious often wear braids.

LONG, WAVY
This hairstyle is long and falls in random waves around the face and shoulders.

BOWL CUT
Geeky or nerdy characters commonly have this cut, as do quiet, reserved characters.

SPIKY
This hairstyle is common in male anime and manga characters. You may find this unkempt hairstyle on young, active characters and heroes.

SHORT CUT
This style is typically found on "nice guy" characters or military/soldier types.

WIDOW'S PEAK WITH LONG BANGS
A widow's peak is hair that grows toward the center of the forehead and forms a V.

The most important factor for drawing straight hair is to use straight lines, of course! With this short, straight cut, the red arrows show the sections and outlines that should be straight. The style may vary when outside elements are at play, such as wind, or if the character is moving swiftly in one direction.

tip

After learning to draw a variety of hairstyles, experiment by combining styles or making up your own creations!

Notice how our green-haired boy has varying lengths of hair that "sprout" in different directions. Hair grows from the crown of the head and falls downward. And the longer the hair, the heavier it is. Drawing sections of hair in different sizes and having them fall naturally is important here.

This chibi girl has long blonde hair that appears to be blowing in the wind or moving as she turns her head. Long, sweeping lines suggest waves in her hair, and the pieces separate into different sections toward the tips.
Drawing hair that moves in one piece and in one direction would look stiff and unnatural.

EXERCISE YOUR CREATIVITY!
On a piece of paper, draw a variety of squiggles, zigzags, and swirls; then use those lines to create a bunch of unique hairstyles.

When drawing curly hair, think of what happens to a straight ribbon when you curl it with scissors. The ribbon's length remains the same, but the ribbon appears shorter because it forms curls. Check out the sketch of the curled hair and note the red spiral arrow next to it. Can you see the direction of the arrow inside the curl?

chibi cLothing

One of the best parts of drawing chibis is creating their identities through clothing and accessories. The options are limitless, so summon your inner fashion designer and dress your chibis in a way that's as awesome as the stories surrounding them!

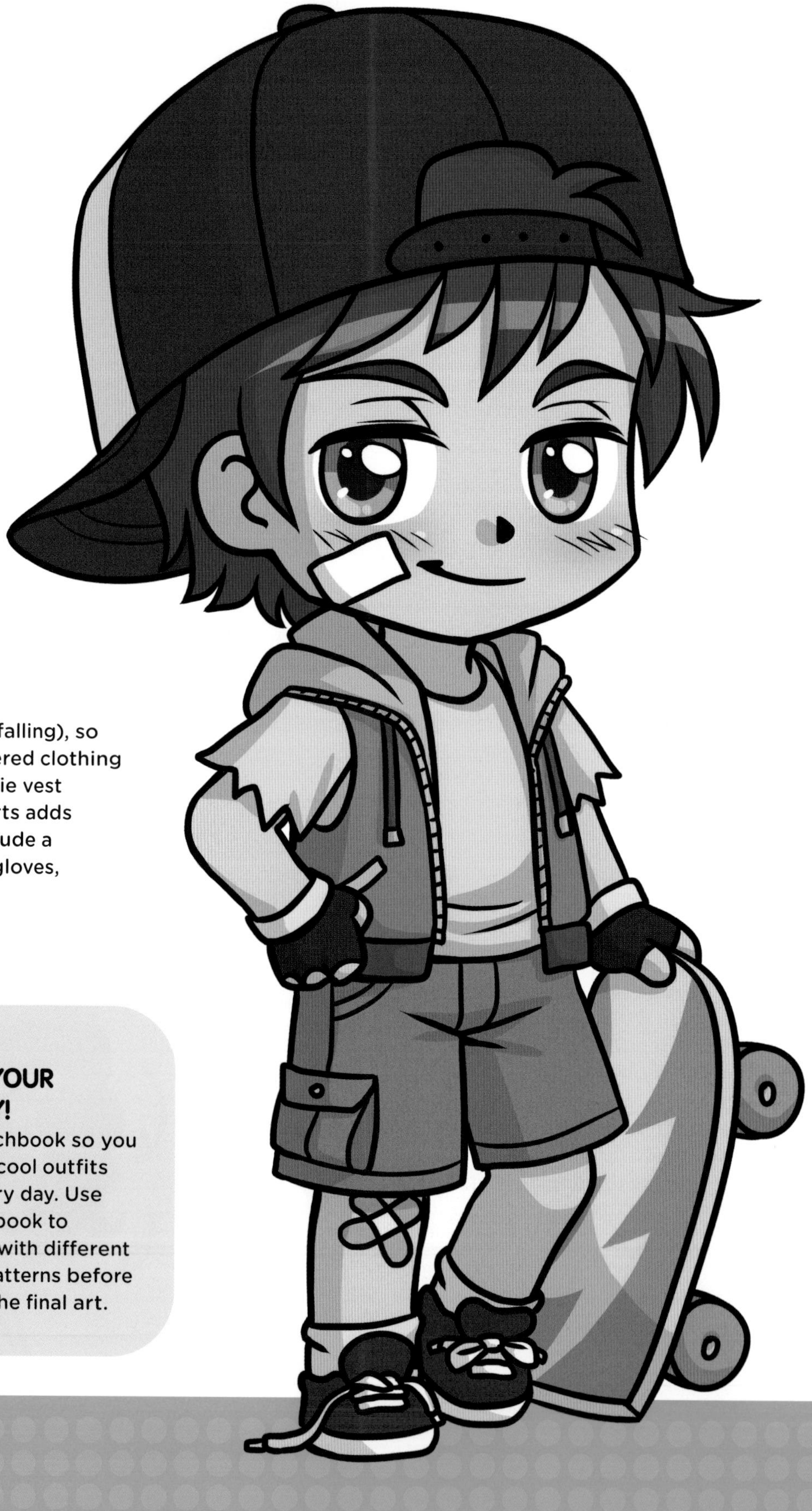

SKATER BOY

Skaters are constantly moving (and falling), so dressing a skater boy in casual, tattered clothing is a good start. A green zip-up hoodie vest layered over the shirt and khaki shorts adds a sporty vibe. Other accessories include a backwards baseball cap, fingerless gloves, red sneakers, and a few bandages.

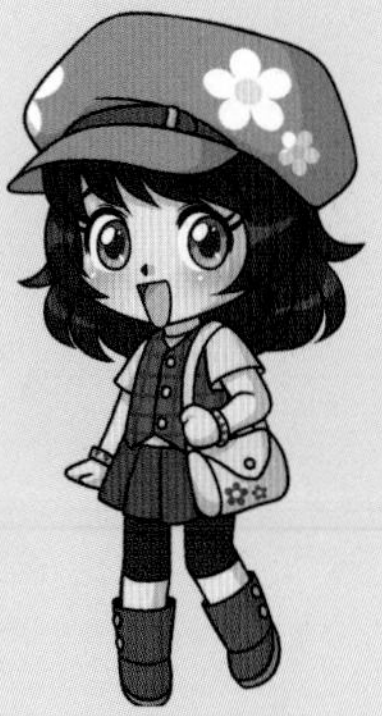

EXERCISE YOUR CREATIVITY!

Keep a sketchbook so you can doodle cool outfits you see every day. Use your sketchbook to experiment with different looks and patterns before diving into the final art.

BOOKWORM GIRL

This bookworm's clothes are neat, prim, and ironed to perfection. She wears a long-sleeved white blouse with a collar and a purple sweater vest in an argyle pattern. A simple tube skirt, knee-high stockings, and a pair of black Mary Janes add a bit of traditional charm.

tip

Drawing an argyle pattern is easy. The pattern consists of stacked diamond shapes in alternating shades, with contrasting lines moving through the centers in "X" shapes. Try making your own color combinations and see how many argyle patterns you can come up with.

tops

RUFFLED BLOUSE
Short puffy sleeves make this top more cute than formal, and frilly lace trim adds pretty detail. Finally, the small polka-dot pattern makes a sweet but subtle statement.

LAYERED
This undershirt is a simple V-neck in a pink-and-white striped pattern. Layered over it is a lavender top tied at the bust, with gently flowing ruffles.

SLEEVELESS
A sleeveless top is a cute option for girls. Instead of drawing a straight hem, add a scalloped edge for more style. Scalloped lace embellishes the straps, and a cute polka-dot pattern and pink bow complete the look.

EMPIRE WAIST
An empire waist is when the dividing line of a top or dress is placed directly under the chest instead of at the waist. This yellow short-sleeved shirt with a green empire-waist top layered over it is super cute.

tip

Explore patterns and decorations to enhance clothing, but be aware that using too many details may make an outfit appear busy and mismatched. Color is another key component to consider. Use a color wheel to experiment with complementary color combinations. (See "Color Basics" on page 12.)

RAGLAN

This style of shirt is white with a collar and three-quarter sleeves in the same solid color. It's popular for activewear and sports uniforms. Add a large number to the front and back to create a jersey.

FLANNEL

An open flannel shirt layered over a solid-colored T-shirt is a great look for boys. Look closely at the pattern on this flannel: It consists of straight lines crossing each other vertically and horizontally. Easy!

PIRATE SHIRT

Who said your characters have to look modern all the time? This pirate shirt has long, billowy sleeves; a wide collar; and an open V-neck tied with a string. A plain brown sash cinches at the waist.

SHIRT & BLAZER

For a dressy look, pair a collared shirt with a pinstriped blazer. Letting the shirtsleeves show slightly creates a nice balance of color. The handkerchief inside the blazer pocket and the striped tie complete the look.

bottoms

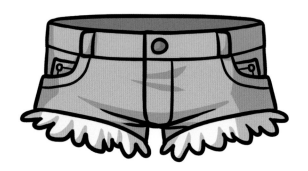

PLEATED SKIRT

This skirt's unique pleated cut leaves room for lots of experimentation. Play around with the width of each pleat, and try using different patterns, such as the argyle pattern on page 29. You can vary the length as well.

SHORT SHORTS

Draw a pair of jeans cut off at the top part of the thigh. For detail, draw in seam lines at the waist and pockets, and fray the hems. Layering these over colorful or patterned leggings creates a hip, modern look.

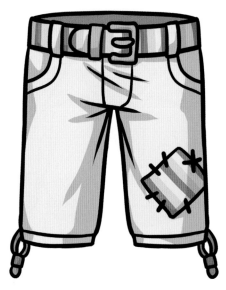

SKIRT & SARONG

This sarong is layered over a long skirt. Pair with a cute bikini top, and your chibi character is set for a fun day at the beach!

CAPRI PANTS

The length of Capri pants is about mid calf. This cute pair has a fun striped belt and matching patch. Beads adorn the drawstrings on each leg cuff. Add some sandals and a sleeveless top, and you have a fresh ensemble for a sun-loving chibi.

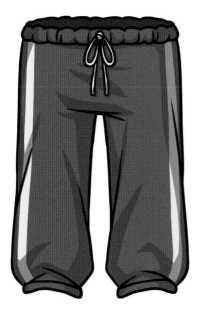

SWEATPANTS
Traditional sweatpants include a drawstring waistline, an elasticized hem at the ankle, and a stripe going down the side of each leg. Maybe your character wears one pant leg rolled up higher than the other. Or perhaps your character requires an extra-fancy pair because he/she is a professional athlete.

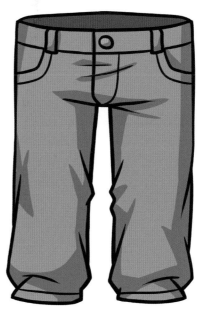

JEANS
Jeans are versatile and come in a variety of cuts and colors. They're also fun to draw because of the many details you can add, like seams, belt loops, and buttons.

EXERCISE YOUR CREATIVITY!
Pair some of the tops from the previous section with some of the bottoms here. Don't forget to dig through your own closet in search of other styles that might suit your chibi characters.

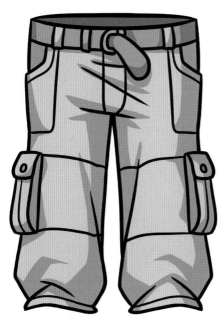

CARGO PANTS
Cargo pants come in a wide range of colors and have pockets on the sides, rear, and on the legs. Some also include a belt. Make sure not to draw cargo pants too form-fitting. They are meant to be baggy.

"CAMO" SHORTS
These camo (short for camouflage) shorts are longer than typical shorts, with hems that fall right above the knee. Like with jeans, draw in seam lines at the waist, on the hems of the legs, and on the pockets. Be sure to add some roomy pockets on each side.

outerwear

WINTER COAT
The waist disappears when chibifying this chilly weather coat, and the torso assumes a bell shape. The sleeves bulge in the center, to make the jacket appear extra thick. Other details include seams on the cuffs, hemlines, and side pockets.

HOODIE
The zipper makes this casual, lightweight jacket enjoyable to draw. You can choose from a variety of styles and vary the width of the zipper itself. Like the winter coat, the chibi version of this hoodie features a bell-shaped torso. The sleeves puff out slightly, and gather at the wrists. Add dangling drawstrings at the top!

TRENCH COAT
A trench coat cut is typically double-breasted, with a broad collar and a belt or sash that ties around the waist. Try giving this coat a slightly subtler bell-shaped torso, taking the belted waist into account. Don't think you're restricted to the beige color. Bright yellow, red, and black are equally acceptable.

PARKA
Parkas are thick, hooded jackets often lined with faux fur for staying warm in frosty temperatures. They come in a variety of colors and styles, with features including extra-warm down, heavy cotton, and round and hook/claw buttons.

footwear

SNEAKERS
Sneakers come in all shapes, sizes, and patterns. Chibi shoes are simplified and compact.

HIGH HEELS
A tiny wedge under each shoe implies the chibi is wearing heels. The arch between the heel and toes is absent in chibi heels.

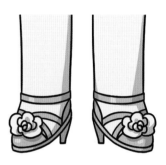

WINTER BOOTS
Because boot styles are sometimes chunky, boot-wearing chibi feet may appear chunky too. That's okay!

SANDALS
The length of the foot is short in the chibi sandals, and the length of the strap is short also.

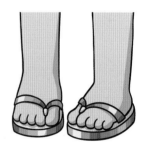

STEEL-TOED BOOTS
This rugged footwear is for tough characters, especially serious, dark fighter-types. There are two belts, a zipper, and a steel-toe with studs on each boot.

EXERCISE YOUR CREATIVITY!
A great way to practice drawing shoes is to draw your own! Try sketching them in a normal-sized style first. Then draw them chibi style.

hats

BASEBALL CAP
Characters can wear this hat forward, backward, sideways, or tilted for different effects. When drawing it in chibi style, make the brim a bit shorter, or else it'll appear too long compared to your chibi's face. For a customized look, create a unique emblem for the front.

KNIT CAP
This cozy winter accessory looks great in solid colors or fun patterns. As you sketch, experiment with proportions: the size of the pom-poms and the length of the ear flaps, for example. The key to drawing these caps is to keep the lines around the edges smooth and curved.

COWBOY HAT
Drawing a sheriff or ranch hand? A cowboy hat is a must. Study a cowboy hat, and you'll see how the brim slopes down in the front and back, and then curls up on the sides. Try changing the colors and adding a flower or ribbon.

SUN HAT
For this casual sunhat, draw a round dome for the top and a brim that extends out and slopes down at the sides. Creating the woven straw texture is easy. A simple crisscross pattern is all you need.

PAGEBOY CAP
The top of this cap is big and loose; it slopes over the edges when worn. Draw basic shapes for a baseball cap, and then draw the cap portion as if you're drawing a deflated balloon.

bags

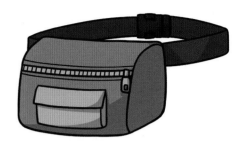

FANNY PACK

To create this travel-friendly bag, begin by drawing a belt. Next, attach a small pouch. The pouch doesn't always have to be in front; it can be on either side or even on the back of the character. Add pockets and zippers as needed.

BACKPACK

This plump little backpack features two compartments. Have fun decorating yours with zippers and seams, but keep things simple. Challenge yourself to draw school backpacks, camping backpacks, laptop bags, or whatever inspires you.

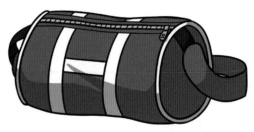

DUFFEL BAG

A duffel bag is perfect for sporty chibi characters, including boxers, karate students, cheerleaders, and gymnasts. Draw a cylindrical shape for the base, and then decorate it with seam lines, zippers, and a strap.

MESSENGER BAG

This bag comes in all shapes and sizes. Start with a basic square, but round the edges. Decorate it with seam lines, patches, zippers, pockets, and straps. Embellish it with butterfly patches, or add a keychain charm hanging from one of the straps.

PURSE

Purse styles range from clutch bags to hobo bags. Our example is a pocketbook purse, which is usually square-shaped with a long, thin strap attached with loops or buckles. Definitely try out different patterns and embellishments!

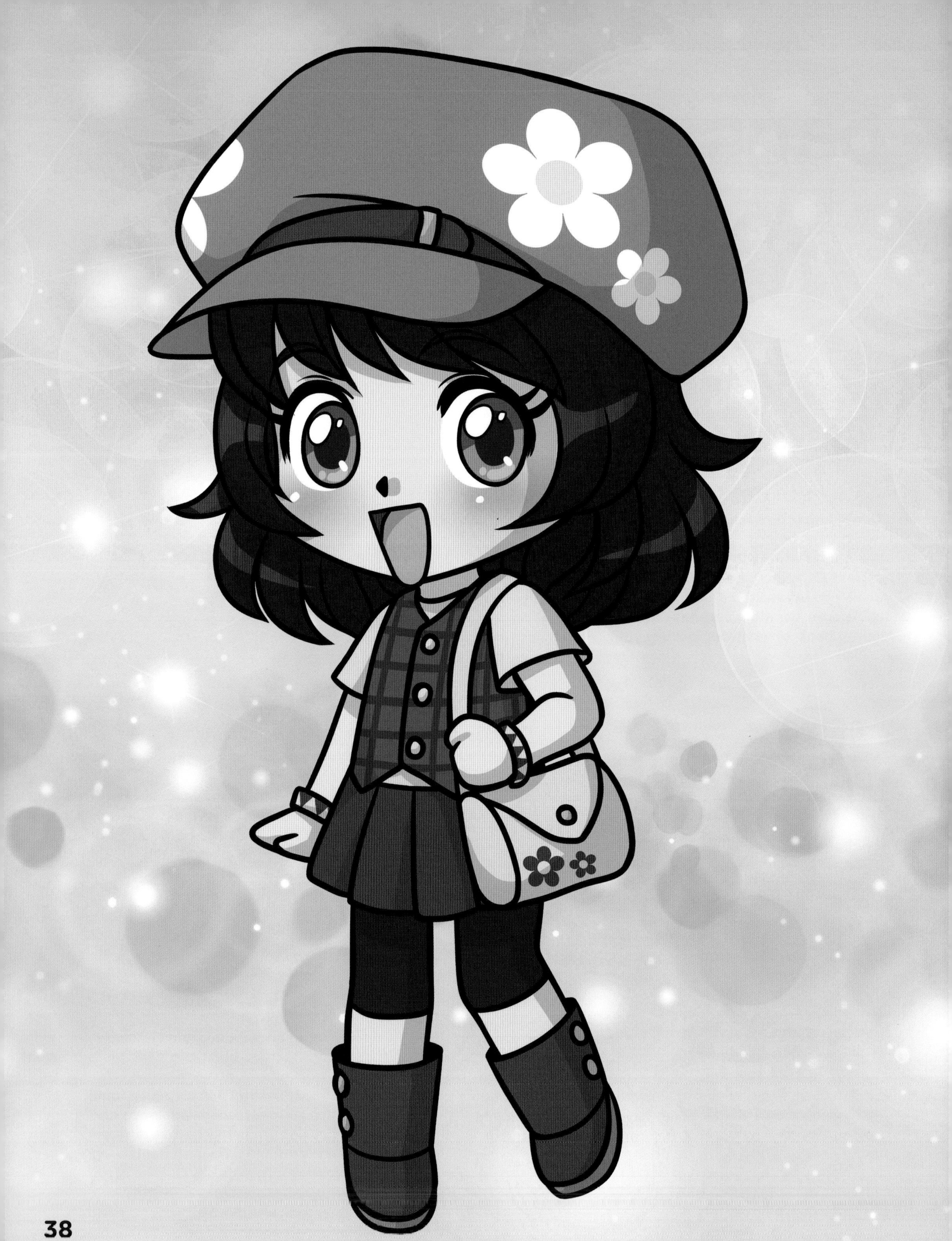

chapter 2
chibi
characters

baby chibi

1

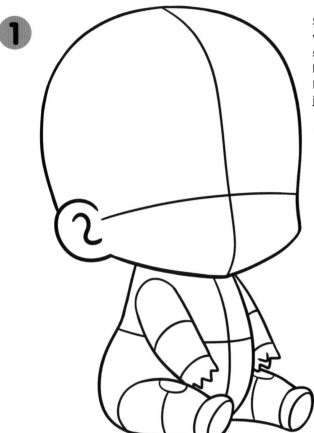

Starting with the basic shapes, draw the head so it's very round. Next, draw the body as a large potato sack shape. Make the bottom portion larger so the baby appears to be firmly planted on the ground. Babies already have short, chubby arms and legs, so just simplify them. Then add tiny hands and feet.

2

tip

Infants have baby fat on their arms and legs, which make them even more cute. Some babies are born with lots of hair; others are born with none. Familiarize yourself with these details, so you know what to add when drawing a baby chibi.

Give the baby large, curious eyes. Don't forget to place the features low on the face to emphasize the large forehead. Add a simple one-piece bodysuit. Finally, draw a round pacifier and a little curl of hair.

3

Time for color! Our baby has light blue eyes and wears a pink and yellow onesie. Add shading to identify the light source as coming from the front-right side. Add dark blue pupils so the eyes appear bright and curious. Also add a light blush to give the baby rosy cheeks.

kid chibi

1

Start with the basic shapes. To make the chibi look like a kid, use a combination of standard chibi and mini-chibi features: a large head, small body, and small hands and feet.

2

tip

Experiment giving your characters of different ages interesting personalities. How about a baby ninja or a superhero grandpa?

Now draw in the details, starting with the facial features. Dress him in a comfortable T-shirt, shorts, and sneakers with socks. Add a messy hairstyle and a backward baseball cap. The bandage on his knee, slingshot, and untied shoelaces tell viewers even more about this character.

3

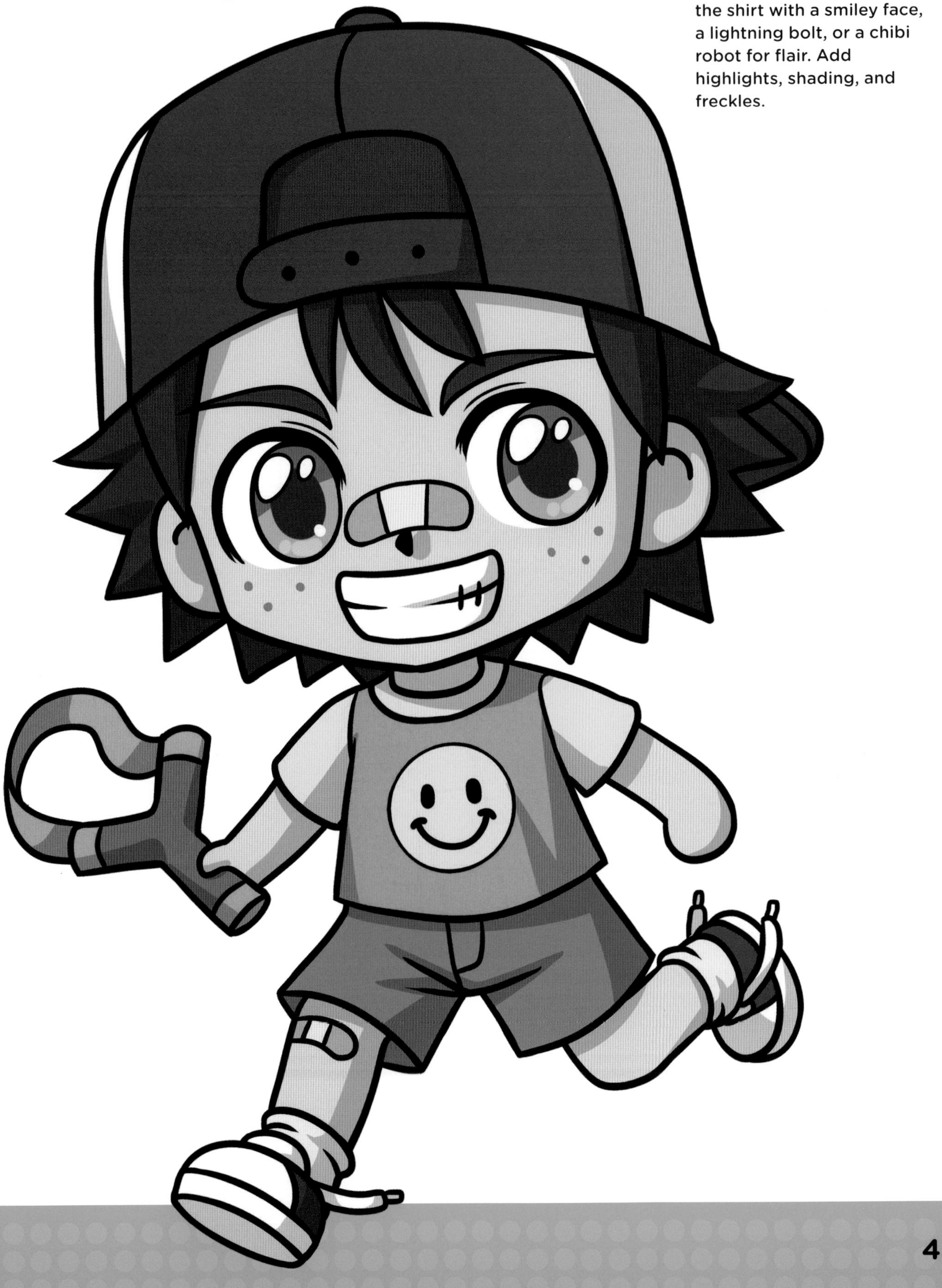

Add bright, energetic colors, such as red, yellow, orange, and blue. Decorate the shirt with a smiley face, a lightning bolt, or a chibi robot for flair. Add highlights, shading, and freckles.

adult chibi

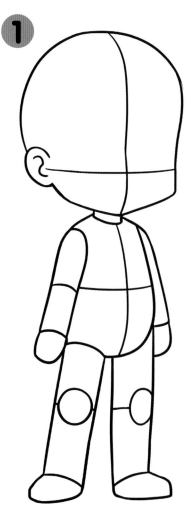

1

Start sketching the basic shapes and guidelines. Draw the arms and feet in a firm stance, but keep the body relaxed.

2

Next, draw the facial expression, which is slightly cranky in keeping with this character's personality. Draw the remaining details, using the guidelines to identify where to draw the clothes and hair.

3

Erase unnecessary sketch lines, and clean up your line art for color.

4

Now add shading to the hair, skin, and clothes. Darken the pupils, adding some brighter highlights to his irises to intensify his stare. Finally, give his hair a few subtle highlights.

senior citizen chibi

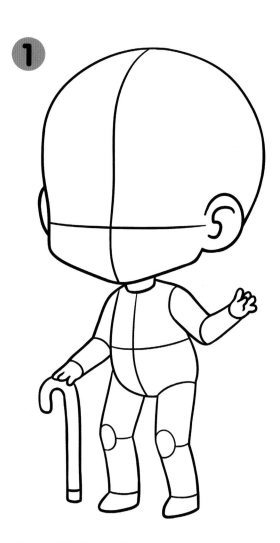

1

2

Start with the basic shapes. Pay attention to how her body hunches over slightly, a telltale sign of her age. Add slight bends in the knees.

Now add the details. Granny's eyes squint slightly, and wrinkles show below her eyes and next to her mouth. Keep clothing simple and comfortable. A traditional bun hairstyle, pearl necklace, cane, and round eyeglasses complete the look.

EXERCISE YOUR CREATIVITY!
Everyday people are invaluable sources of inspiration from which to draw. You'll quickly see that not all kids are super-energetic and not all senior citizens are gray-haired. To get a sense of the differences between people of all ages, do some "people watching" the next time you are in a public place.

3

Add subtle colors for this character. Add highlights to the hair so it looks clean and tidy. Darken the pupils and add highlights to give her gaze more vitality. Finally, create a simple floral pattern on her skirt to spice up the final drawing.

more chibi styles

1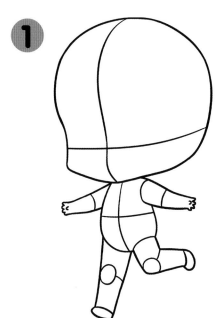

There are many styles of drawing chibis. Let's draw a cross between a typical chibi and a mini-chibi. We combined a large head with a little body. She also has mini hands and feet.

3

Add colors, shading, and highlights.

2

Add the details. Try flipping between this page and the chibi on page 7, and note the differences in style.

tip

Some artists draw super-simplified chibis, with only hair and clothing to distinguish between characters. Other artists design unique eye shapes, head shapes, body shapes, and hairstyles for each character. Experiment by combining various characteristics and elements.

1 Start with the basic shapes and guidelines. Note how large the head is compared to his body. His hands and feet are also large.

3

2 Place the eyes, noting that the eyebrows cover his eyelids. A few thick lines indicate his clothes. The three little marks on the cheeks add a blush. The hands and fingers are large, but they maintain their chibiness because they're thick and round. The feet have a slight cartoony flair.

Lay down your colors and add shading and highlights.

①

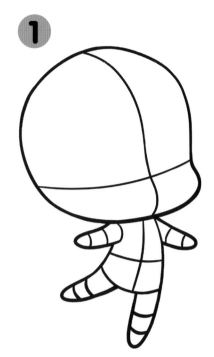

This style is even more simplified than the mini-chibi on page 52! Note her proportions.

③

②

The eyes are two huge dots, the mouth looks like the number "3" on its side, and the details are indicated by simple lines.

As in the previous style exercise, be sure to keep her colors consistent so she looks the same between illustrations. Remember: extremely simplified styles usually work better with less detail.

1

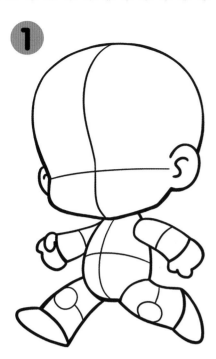

Let's look at one last style. Begin with the basic shapes and guidelines.

2

The eyes are low on his head. He has stylized hair, simply drawn clothes, and mitten-style hands.

3

Make sure to pick the right colors! Don't overdo highlights or shading for simplified styles, or your final drawing will look busy and cluttered.

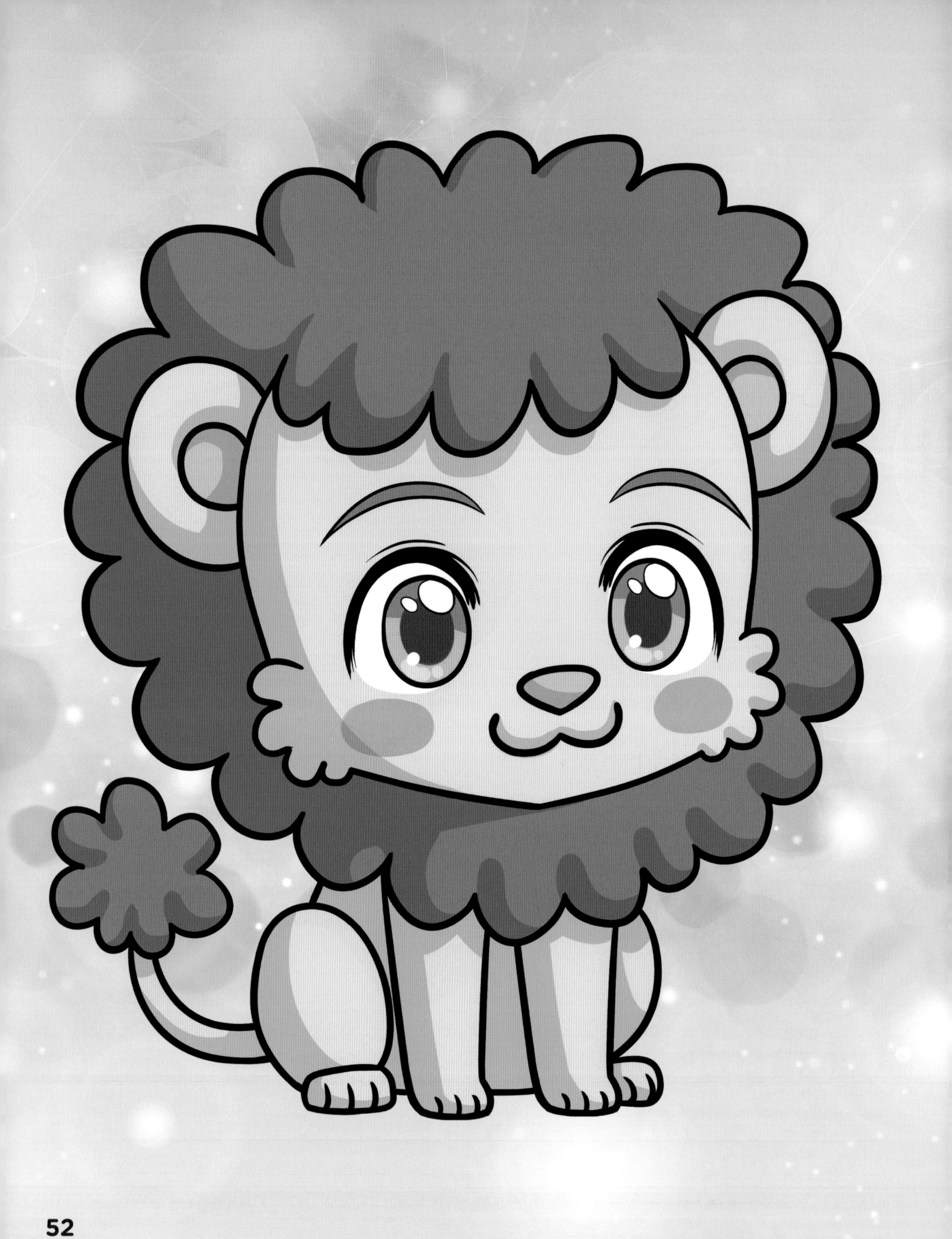

chapter 3
chibi critters

CRITTER faces

Now that you've learned to draw "human" chibis, it's time to draw their chibi critter companions, whose features and characteristics are even more diverse! Some animals have two legs, some have four; some animals have fur, scales, or fins; some have tails, claws, wings, and beaks. Drawing chibi critters is similar to drawing other chibi characters, although the placement of the features varies among species. Most chibi animals have expressive eyes and eyebrows. They're cartoon-like, after all, so they can make all the same expressions a human chibi can make.

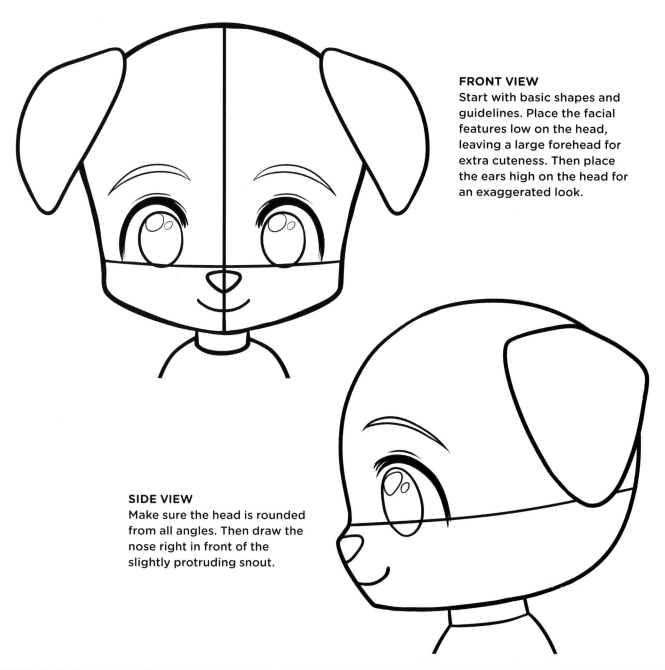

FRONT VIEW
Start with basic shapes and guidelines. Place the facial features low on the head, leaving a large forehead for extra cuteness. Then place the ears high on the head for an exaggerated look.

SIDE VIEW
Make sure the head is rounded from all angles. Then draw the nose right in front of the slightly protruding snout.

¾ VIEW

A three-quarter view is between the front and profile views. Use face guidelines to help place the features accordingly.

BACK VIEW

Double-check that the position of the ears is consistent with the front and profile views.

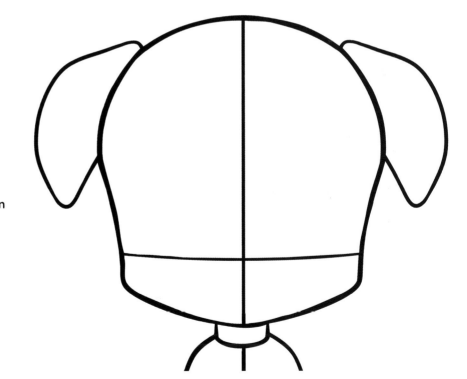

two-legged critters

Many characters from popular cartoons, including Tom and Jerry, Bugs Bunny, and Mickey Mouse, walk on two legs and have human-like traits. Although most animals in the real-life animal kingdom are four-legged, drawing two-legged chibi critters allows for greater fun and experimentation. Proportions for a chibi two-legged critter are similar to that of a basic chibi human character. The head is larger in proportion compared to the rest of the body, which is round, oval, or teardrop shaped and connects directly below the head. The upper limbs are short and stubby, and you can add little thumbs or fingers, if you like. The legs are often slightly larger around the upper thighs.

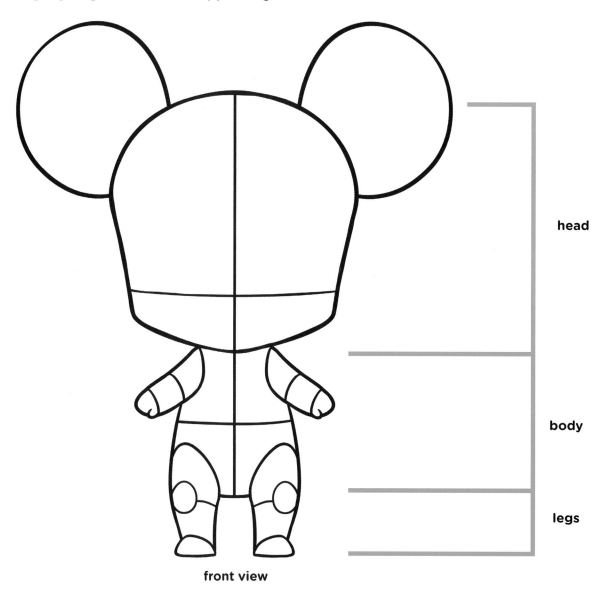

head

body

legs

front view

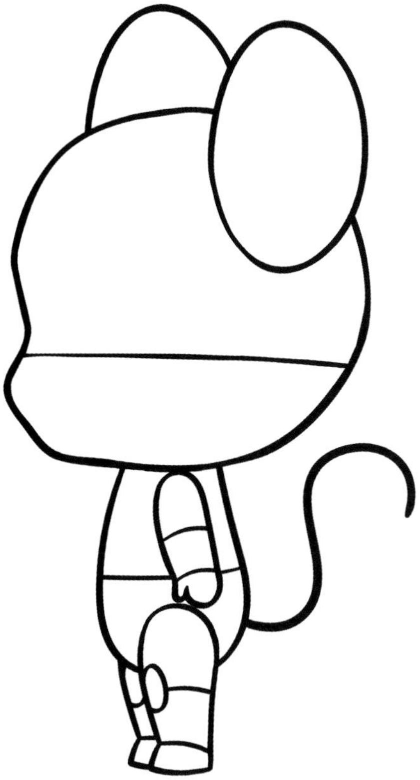

side view

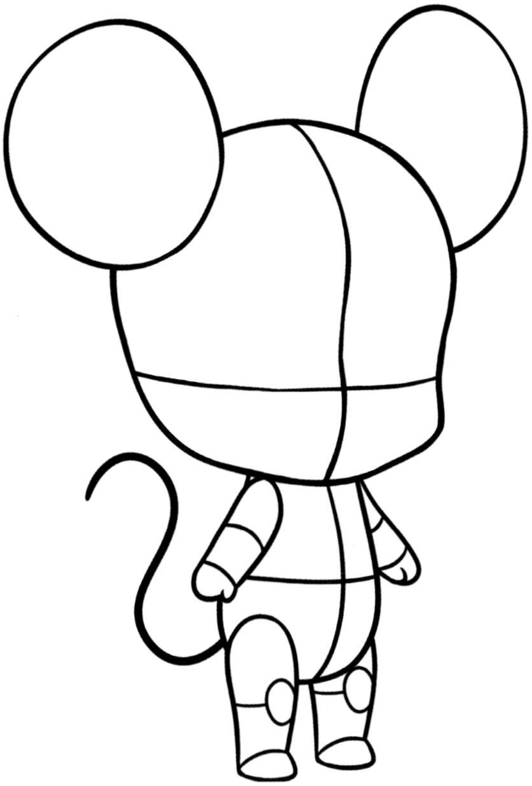

3/4 view

tip

Feel free to experiment with different head and body sizes to see if you can create a personal two-legged critter chibi style.

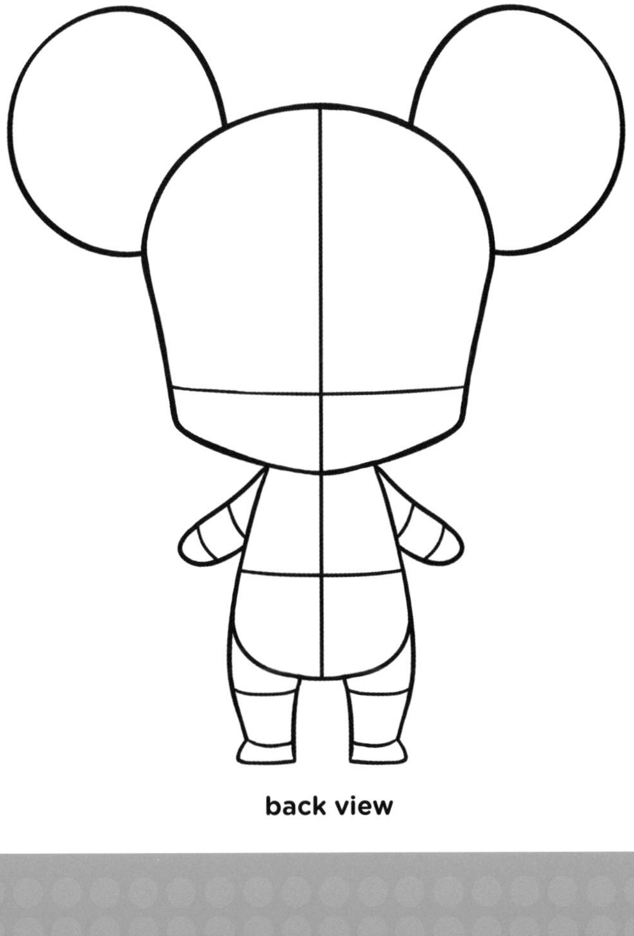

back view

four-Legged critters

Now let's look at the body parts of a four-legged animal. Take a look at the diagrams of a normal dog and a chibified dog below. Notice that the chibi critter's head is much larger than its body, and many of the contour lines are simple. Additionally, the legs are shorter and stouter, and the paws are noticeably smaller—and very cute!

Head
Ear
Tail
Muzzle
Back
Shoulders
Elbow
Thigh
Upper arm
Lower thigh
Forearm
Paw

Head
Ear
Muzzle
Back
Tail
Shoulders
Thigh
Upper arm
Lower thigh
Forearm
Paw
Elbow

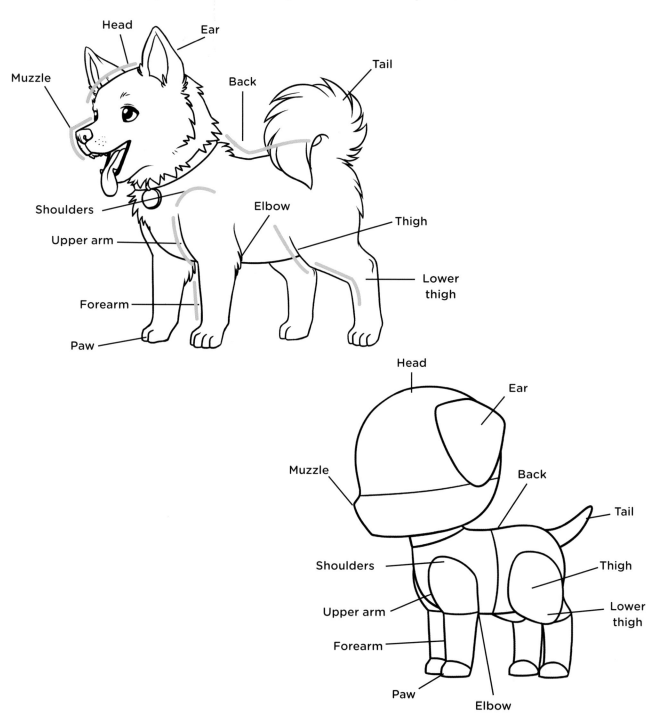

You can draw four-legged chibi critters in a variety of poses. Notice again how the shape of the head changes with each angle and that even when the angles change, the character still appears to be the same shape, height, and size from all views.

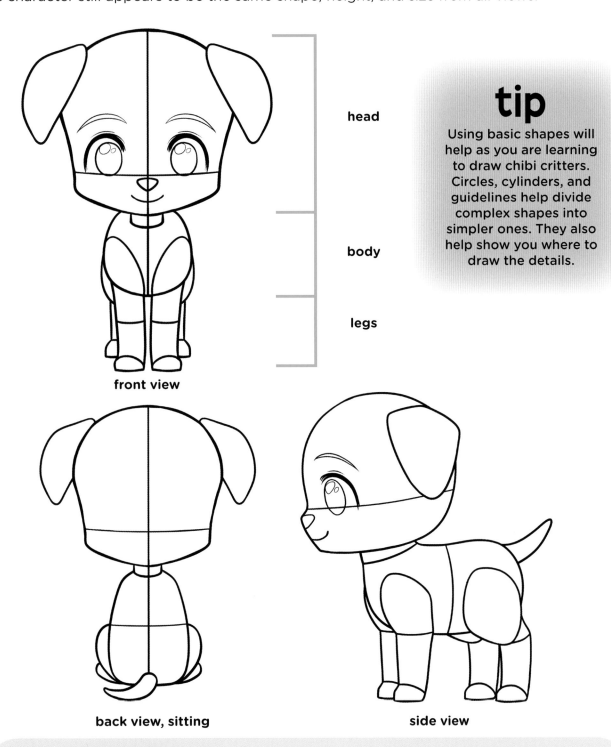

head

body

legs

front view

back view, sitting

side view

tip
Using basic shapes will help as you are learning to draw chibi critters. Circles, cylinders, and guidelines help divide complex shapes into simpler ones. They also help show you where to draw the details.

READY TO PRACTICE?
Use the templates on pages 82–95 to practice drawing chibi critters in many different poses. You can either scan the templates to your computer and print them out or photocopy them from the book.

dog

NORMAL DOG

Shiba Inu dogs have trim faces with long snouts and large, pointy ears that are always erect. Their big eyes reflect their dutiful spirit. They generally have strong, stout midsections; short coats; and a distinctive tail with longer fur that curls toward the body.

For this chibi Shiba Inu, first draw the large head, and add your horizontal and vertical guidelines. Now draw the basic shapes for the legs, along with guidelines indicating the joints. Note the small paws, which make the legs appear tapered.

Add the eyes, exaggerating them to look meaningful. Simplify the mouth, and add a tongue. Draw small tufts of fur in select areas. Now draw two tiny lines on each paw to identify the toes. Then give the dog a small collar with an exaggerated dog tag. Refine the details as you draw the curled tail.

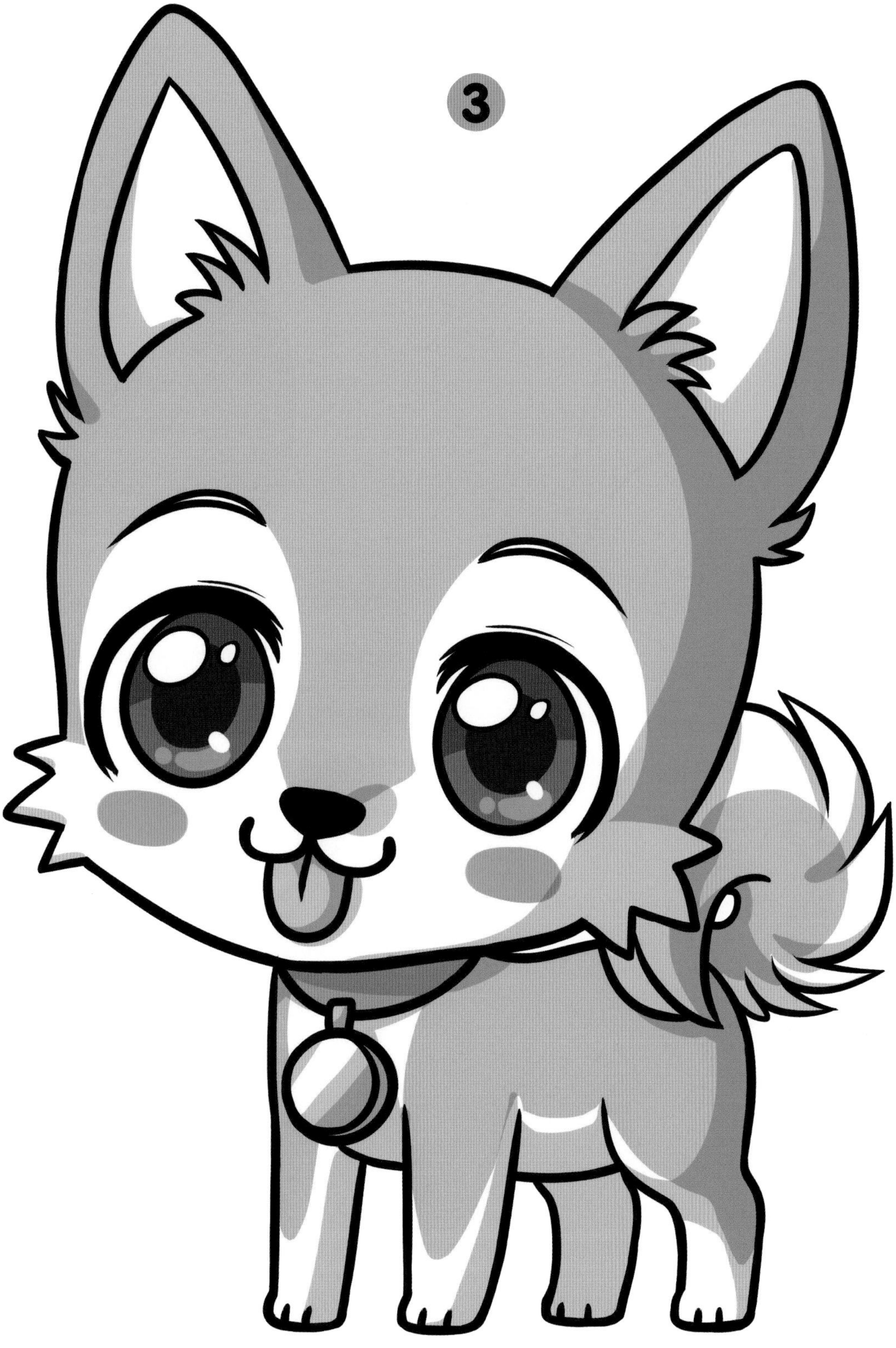
3

Shade and highlight time! The light source is from the upper left corner, so shadows are on the dog's left side. Add highlights to the eyes and darken the pupils. Then add gleaming highlights to the dog tag for a metallic look. Lastly, make the cheeks blush.

cat

NORMAL CAT

Cats have sleek bodies, dainty paws, and tails that swish with their feelings and reflect their grace and agility. But their key feature is large, intense eyes with pupils that go from slits to big black dots. They have short snouts and long whiskers. Ears and tails vary in size and shape depending on breed.

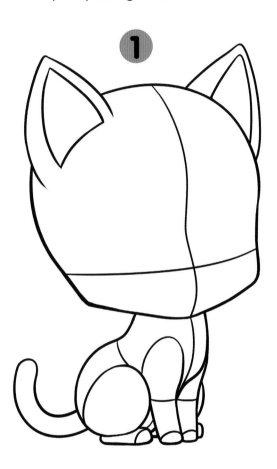

When drawing this tabby cat's body, try to maintain the graceful arch of the back in the sitting position. Simplify the arms and legs, and add guidelines at the joints. The paws should look especially small and delicate. Make the tail shorter and fatter for a cartoonish effect.

Add the facial features, and then add tufts of fur to the inside of the ears, on the cheeks, and on the chest to imply fluffiness. Next, draw short lines on the front and back paws for the toes. Draw whiskers, and don't forget the collar and bell!

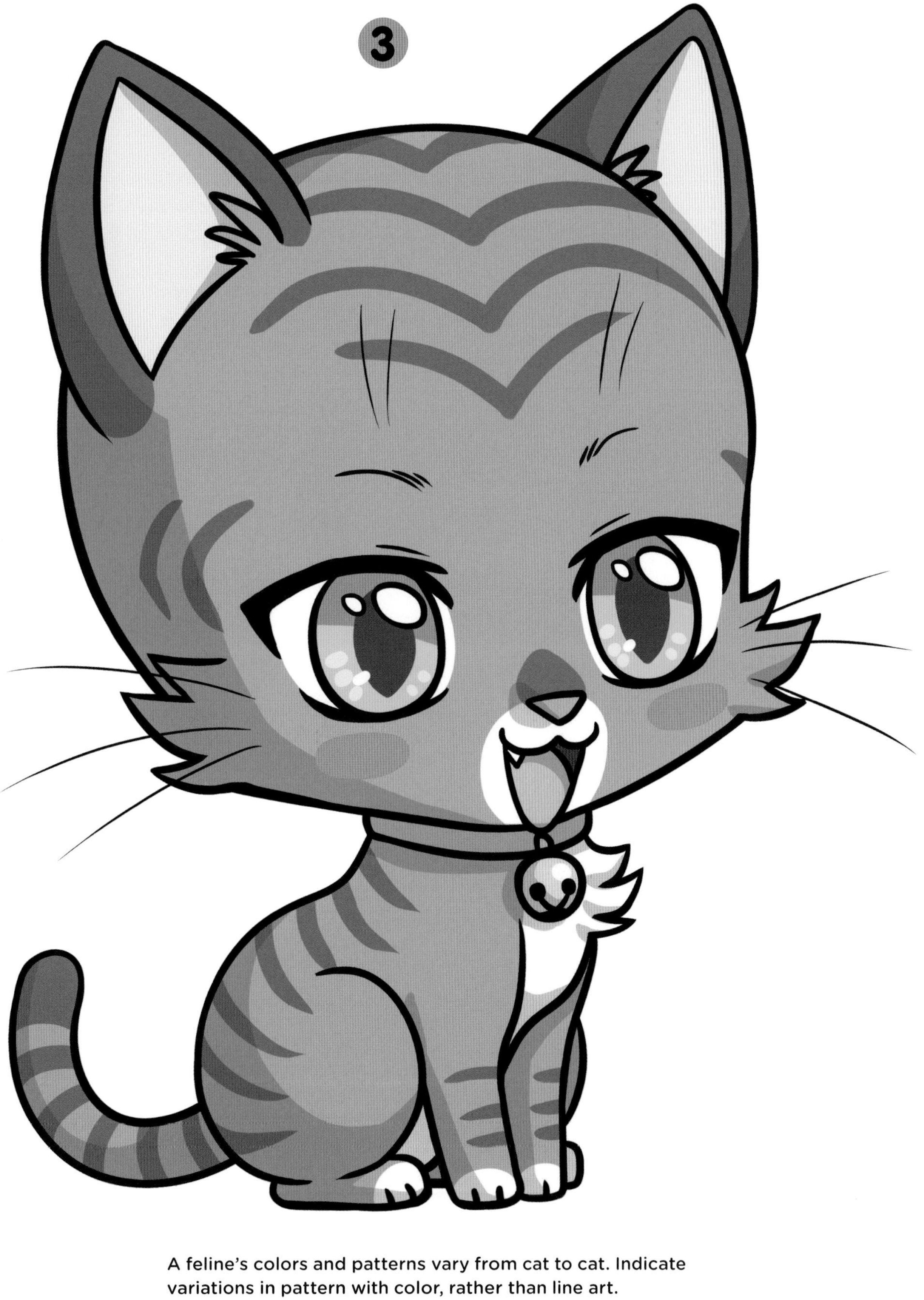

A feline's colors and patterns vary from cat to cat. Indicate variations in pattern with color, rather than line art.

bird

NORMAL BIRD

Because a bird's anatomy is so different from other animals, you must approach its chibi transformation differently. The largest part of a bird's body is its oval-shaped midsection that narrows toward the tail feathers. This cockatiel has a small head with a crest of feathers. It also has a small, hook-shaped beak with tiny nostrils. Its eyes are beady and situated toward the sides of the head. When perched, its spindly, scaly toes curl around the branch, and its wings tuck into its body.

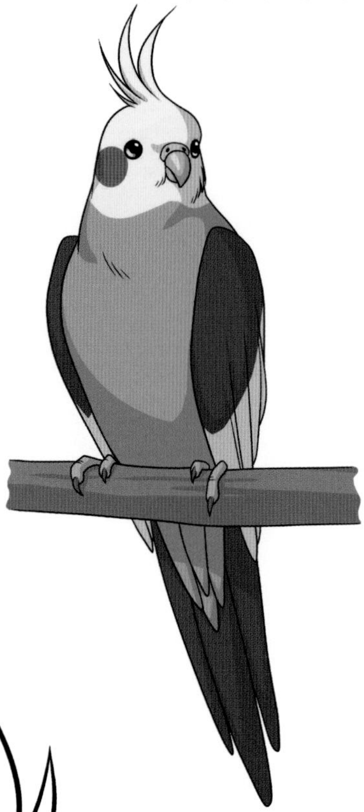

1

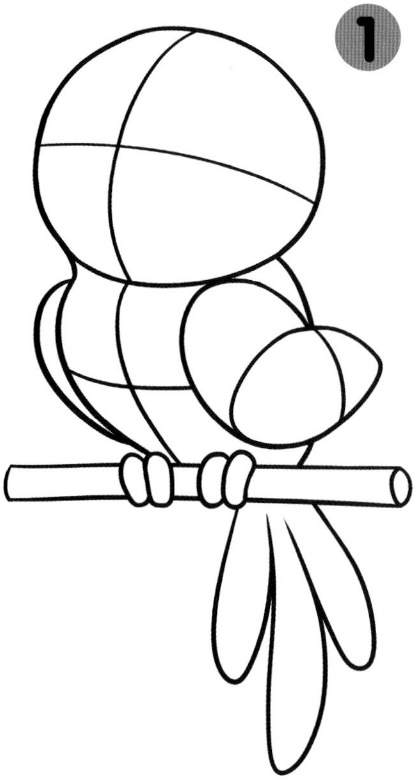

Draw the basic shapes, exaggerating the head to appear large and round. Use guidelines to help maintain correct proportions. Notice the toes, which are plump and rounded, and the simple tail feathers.

2

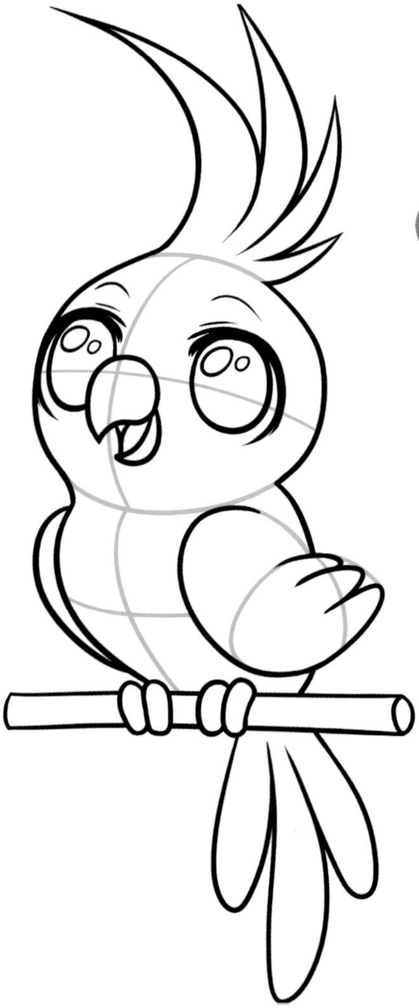

Draw large, round eyes, and tiny eyebrows. Draw a small, simplified beak. Continue adding the details, starting with the crest. Draw a few feathers on the wings.

3

Establish your yellow, gray, and white color zones. Designate a light source and shade the appropriate areas. Make sure the shading follows the shape of the bird's head. Add darker pupils and key highlights to the eyes.

fantasy critters

FLYING BEAR
Start with an ordinary teddy bear; then add fantastical details to make him extraordinary: a purple bobble on his head; a stars and moon emblem on his forehead; large, fluffy white wings; and blue fur on his chest and feet.

DINO-LIZARD
Our imaginary lizard has a dinosaur-like body and unique purple markings on his forehead, eyes, and legs. Purple spikes along his back and tail and a single curved horn add character.

ROUND BIRD
This plump little bird qualifies as a super-chibi. She has an ultra-simplified body (just a circle!); huge, round eyes; a teeny beak; and simple wings, legs, and tail feathers. Her sparkly eyes and the heart on her chest suggest a sweet personality.

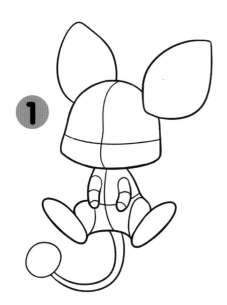

1 This magical creature has rabbit-like attributes: big, fluffy ears; small front limbs; large hind legs; and long, flat feet. Start by drawing the basic shapes.

2 Add the details, including the diamond-shaped gem in the middle of his forehead. He has peg-leg front limbs, and his feet have single pads. Finally, draw cute little wings and a long tail with a tuft of fur on the end.

When shading, note that the light source is coming from the left side. When shading the forehead jewel, use a base color, a darker shading color, and a reflective light color to give it depth and intensity.

3

EXERCISE YOUR CREATIVITY!

Imaginary critters make excellent main characters in a story and even better sidekicks. For example, a girl just discovering her magical powers may need a wise critter guide. For inspiration, think of stories in which imaginary critters play major roles.

critter combos

BUNNY-DOG-RACCOON
This silly critter has the body of a dog, the ears of a bunny, and the tail of a raccoon. He also walks on two legs, not four. Notice how his long ears match the shape of his tail and how lighter fur stripes accent both. He also sports an amber jewel on his forehead. Bright red eyes reflect his fun and fiery personality.

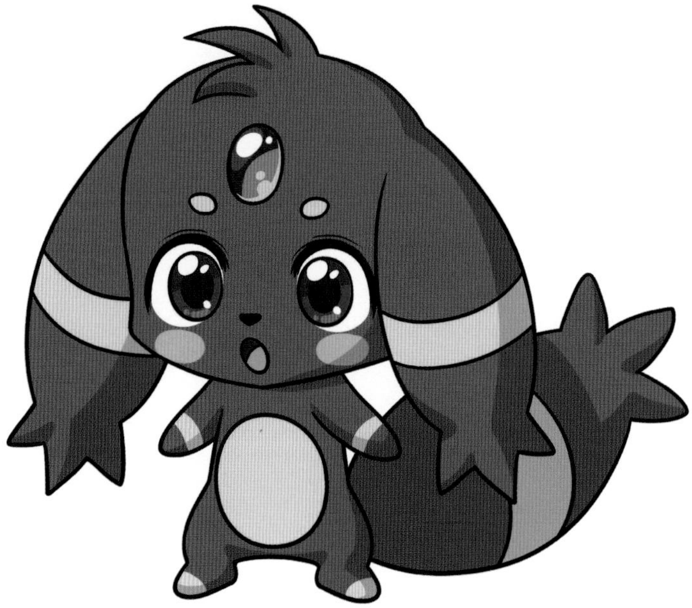

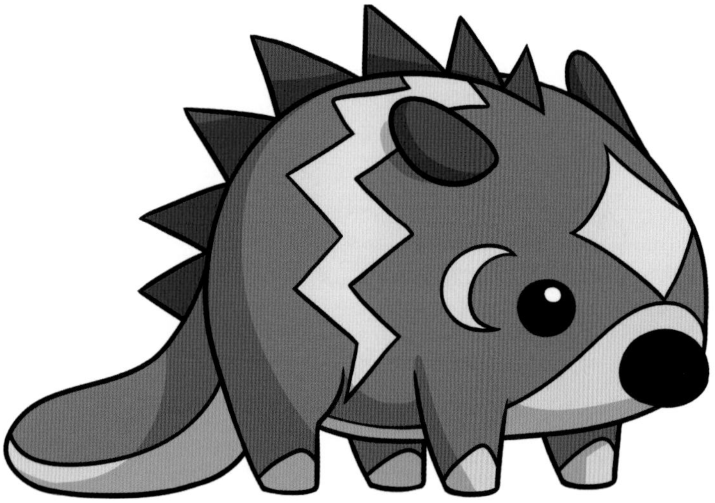

PURPLE PORCUPINE
A large dome-shaped body is this critter's most defining feature, followed by a row of dark purple quills on his back. Vibrant yellow emblems in interesting shapes add contrast to the fantasy-friendly purple tone. He also has a paddle-like beaver's tail and stubby flat feet. His spikes and strong tail indicate this critter might specialize in defending others.

BIRD-DRAGON
This fantasy critter has the body of a dragon and the head, beak, and feathers of a parrot. Bright red scales makes him appear bold and exotic, and his googly eyes hint at a silly personality, despite his fierce colors.

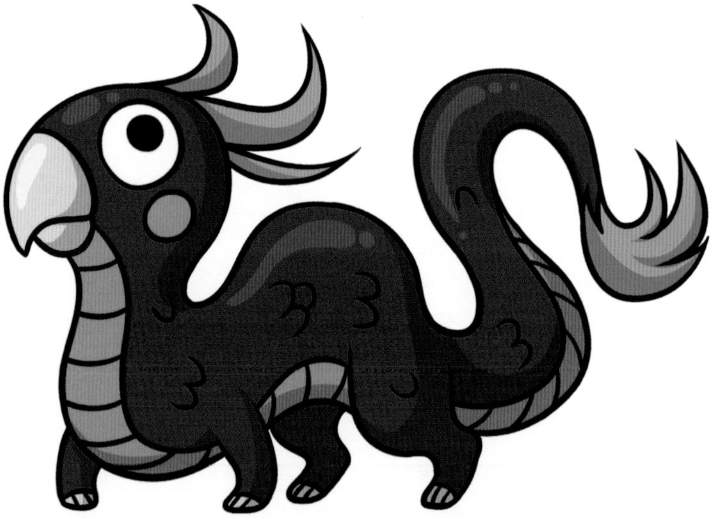

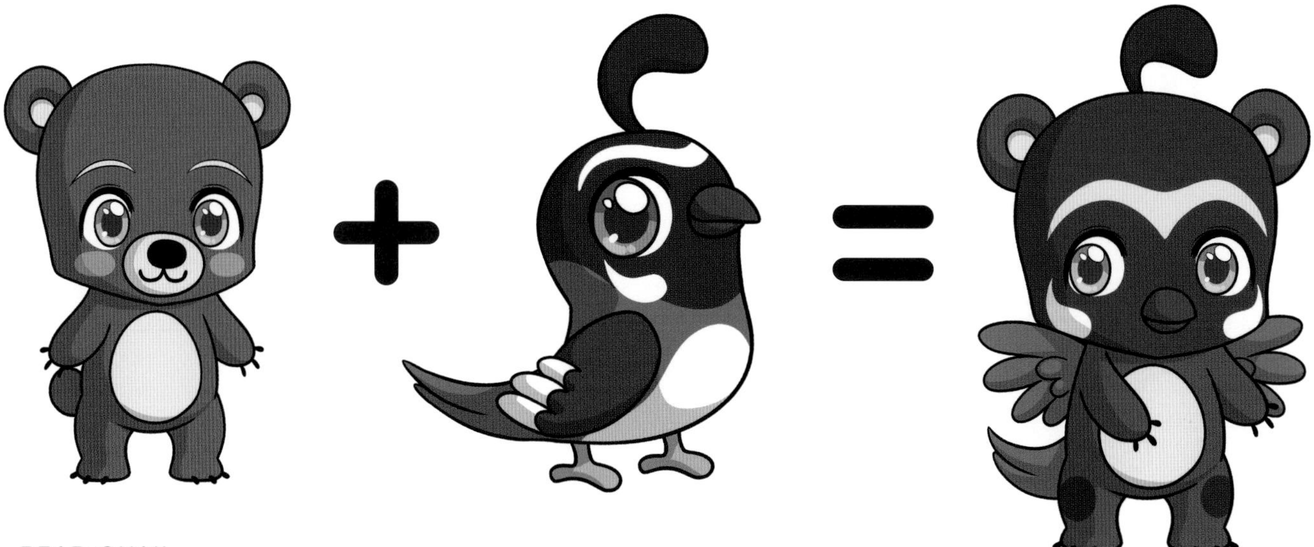

BEAR-QUAIL

Ever wonder what a bear-quail hybrid would look like? Wonder no more! Although our critter has the body shape, heavy fur, round ears, and strong limbs of a bear, he also has key quail features, such as a head plume and feather markings.

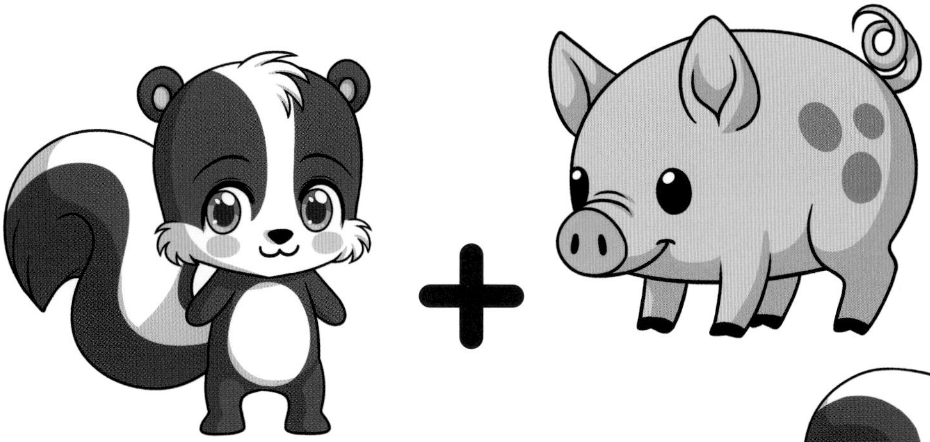

PIG-SKUNK

This critter has the chubby, oval body shape of a pig and the coloring, tail, and fur of a skunk. Little pink spots on the body, as well as rosy cheeks, give this fantastic creature even more charisma.

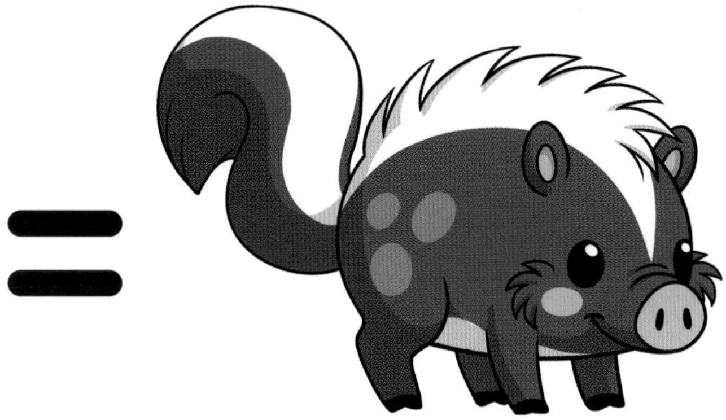

EXERCISE YOUR CREATIVITY!

When combining critters, start by choosing the basic body shape. Do you want your critter to be based mostly off one animal, or would you rather combine shapes from both? Then ask yourself the following questions:

1. How many legs does your critter have?
2. Does your critter fly? If so, does it use wings or does it float?
3. Does your critter have fur, scales, or fins?
4. What colors do you want your critter to be?

chibifying any CRITTER

LION
Our chibi lion has a large head with peg-like limbs and simplified paws. His signature mane and matching tail are rounded and cloud-like so they appear fluffy. The ears are rounded and are drawn a little larger so they don't disappear into the mane.

tip

You can chibify anything! Just remember what defines the basic chibi style: simplification of detail and exaggeration of specific features to emphasize a certain look or characteristic.

CROCODILE
A crocodile's menacing features include a long snout; sharp teeth; beady eyes; razor-sharp claws; and rough, scaly skin. In a chibi rendering, these features are cute, not scary.

SHARK

Turn this fierce ocean beast into a more approachable chibi character. Draw a small, round, football-shaped body and fins with slightly rounded tips. Give him big, friendly eyes and an extra-large toothy grin. Add a few bubbles for effect.

BAT

Bats have large wings covered with thin flaps of skin. This unusual attribute is what you want to emphasize as you begin chibifying. Tiny fangs and a blush on his cheeks show his sweet side!

EXERCISE YOUR CREATIVITY!

Select a critter's most distinctive features to exaggerate in chibi form. Choose a few animals you want to try chibifying. Determine their key features, proportions, and personalities before you start drawing.

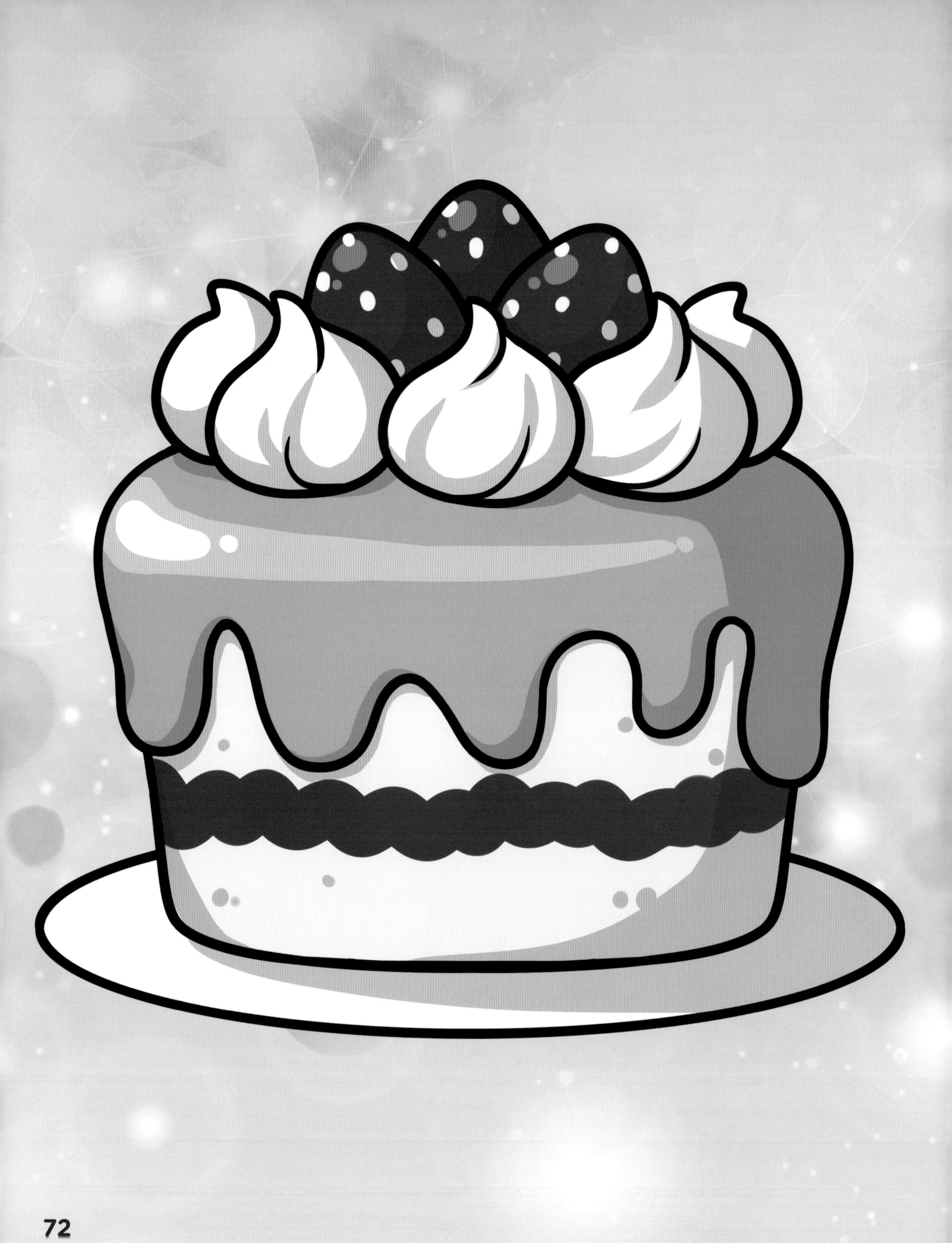

chapter 4

chibi props & scenes

chibi food

Chibi food is enjoyable to draw. Think of the possibilities: a chibi girl in roller skates eating a popsicle or a dashing young chibi waiter serving a tray of goodies. Remember to focus on the primary details of your subject and emphasize them, while omitting unnecessary details. As always, think "cute" and "plump."

SWEET TREATS

Delicious sweet confections like cakes, cookies, tarts, and tea are tons of fun to draw in chibi style. After being simplified, an elaborately decorated cake becomes a plump, cartoonish shape with exaggerated strawberries and whipped cream. You can add intricate detail to the teacup's side and saucer for a dash of elegance. Cookies are super easy to draw, and frosted cupcakes covered in colorful sprinkles add whimsy to the spread.

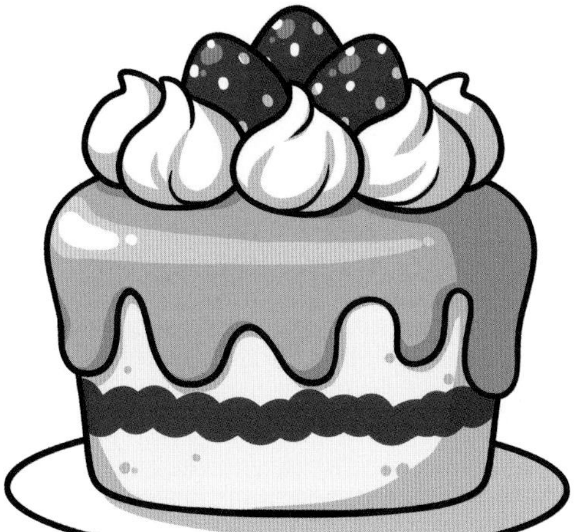

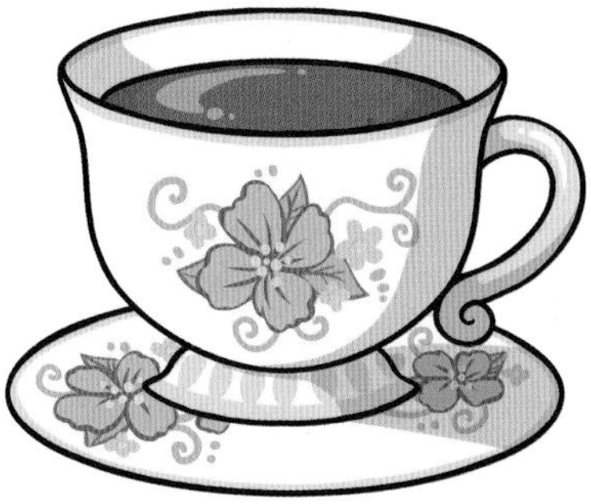

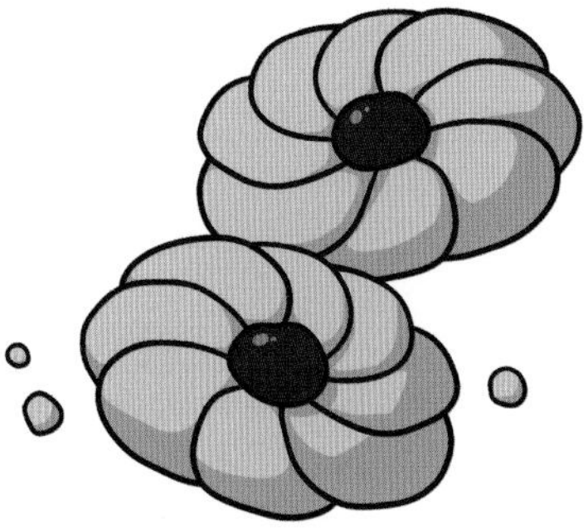

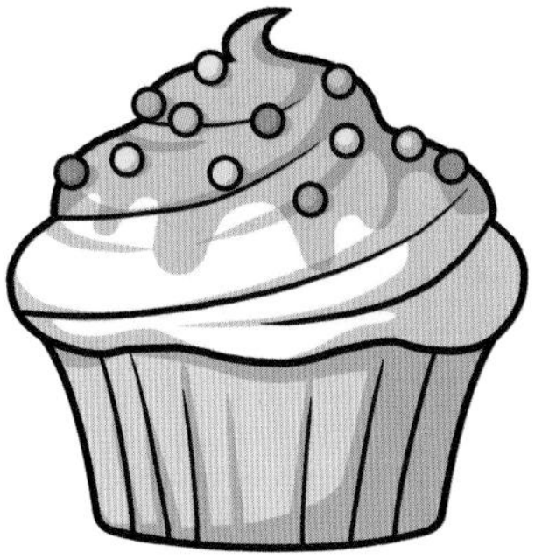

BREAKFAST

There are many ways to interpret breakfast depending on where in the world your characters live. One popular morning meal is a fried egg atop a slice of toast. Riceballs are a common breakfast in anime and manga. An "Octopus" sausage is a tiny hot dog with one end cut to mimic tentacles. They're a staple in bento (lunch boxes) in Japan.

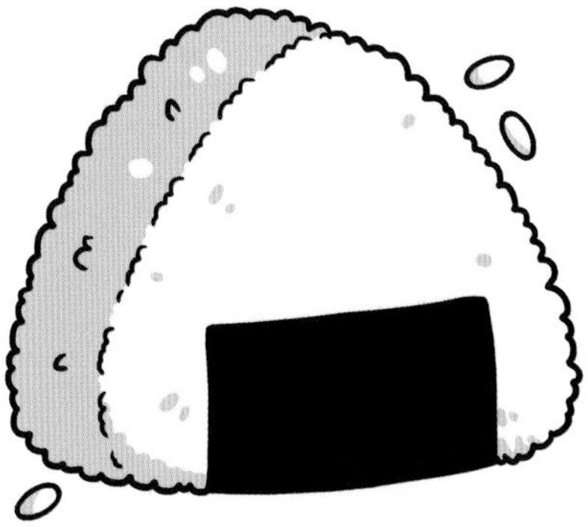

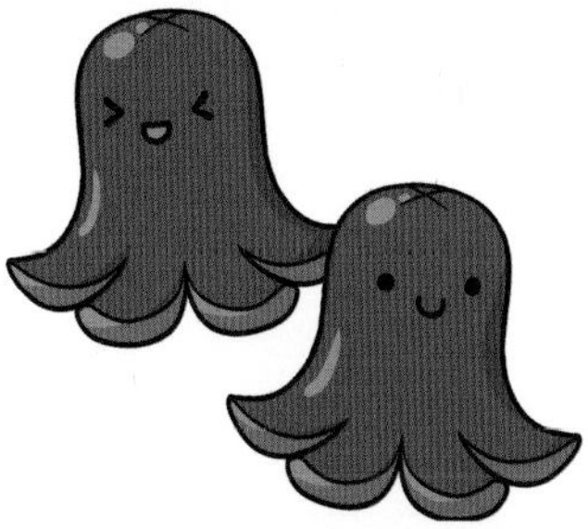

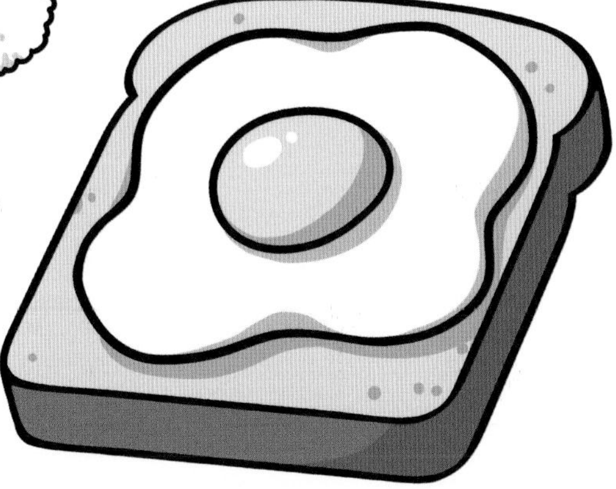

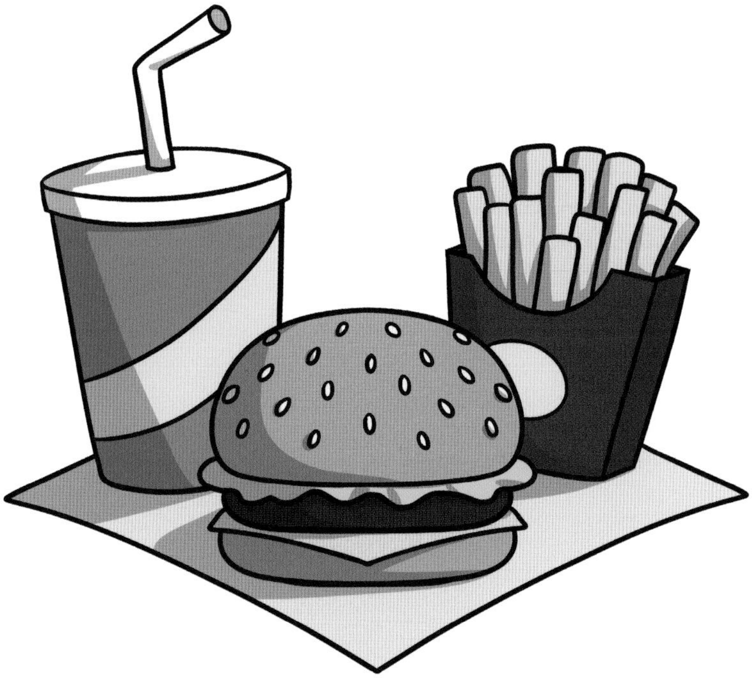

FAST FOOD

Fast food joints: the ideal meeting places for hungry young chibi characters. To draw a burger, begin with round, basic shapes to get the correct proportions. Draw in each detail. Then draw a cylindrical shape for the drink. Add a straw and a design to the cup. Draw a French fry carton and rectangular shapes for the fries.

ICE CREAM

For the sundae, use long oval shapes for the glass and ice cream. Then draw another loose oval guideline for the whipped cream and cherry. For the ice cream cone, sketch two circular shapes for the two scoops of ice cream and a triangular guideline for the cone. Then add the details. For the banana split, add loose basic shapes for the bananas and three circular shapes for the ice cream scoops. Sketch in the whipped cream and cherry.

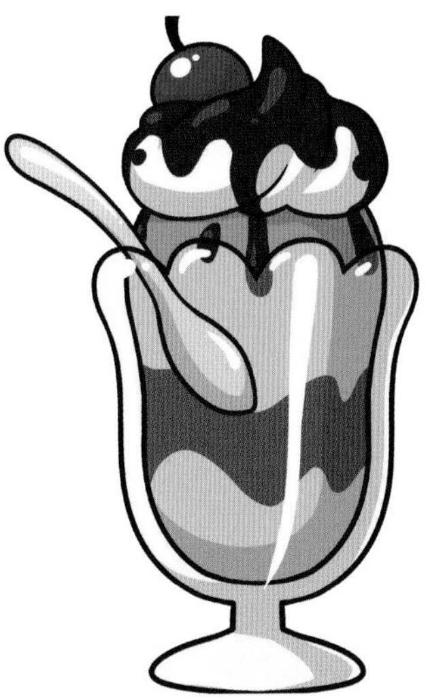

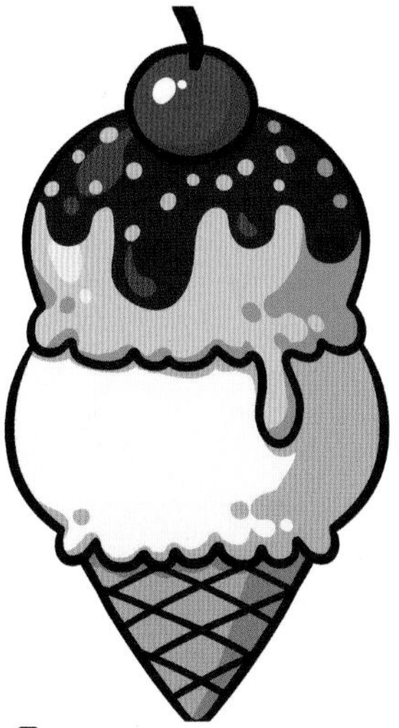

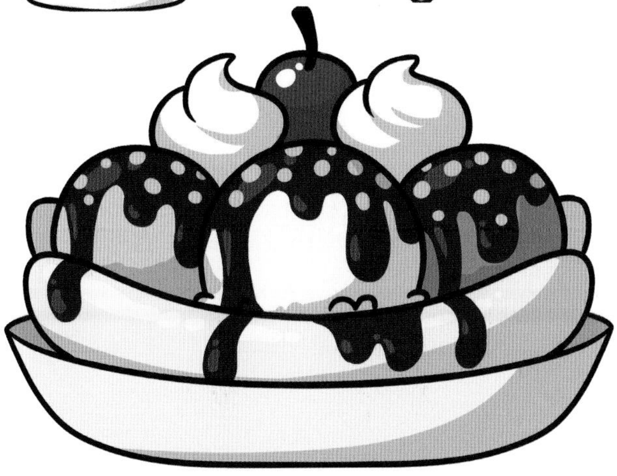

chibi furniture

As you become comfortable drawing in your own chibi style, you may want to create settings and furnishings for your characters. Settings make your art interesting and help tell stories about the characters. When drawing inanimate objects, you still identify and draw the basic shapes. Visualize which details to simplify and which to exaggerate.

CHAIR
The chibi chair is small and chunky, and it resembles a child's toy chair. Notice the exaggerated thickness of the chair.

BED
The chibi bed is short and stout. See how the sides slant outward at the top? This is a stylistic choice to make the bed look more cartoonish. Exaggerating the size of the balls adorning the frame serves the same purpose.

TELEVISION
The chibi TV has rounded corners and bulging sides. It is slightly wider on top, with a wacky zigzag antenna.

LAMP

The lamp's chibi transformation is as simple as making it shorter and fatter, especially the stand and base. The sides on the lampshade curve in for a cartoonish look. Finally, exaggerate the chain so the ball links are fatter.

COUCH

The back of the couch and the arms are more rounded. The couch is thicker and slants outward for a cartoonish effect. Notice how the seat cushions appear uneven. The pillows are fluffier to make them cuter.

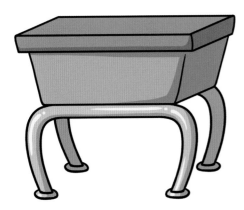

SCHOOL DESK

In chibi style, the top of the desk is thicker and the sides are angled. The legs and horizontal support are also thicker and rounded. Challenge yourself to draw a chibi chair behind this desk, with a chibi character sitting in it.

DRESSER

Like in previous examples, begin by distorting the appearance, making the dresser wider at the top and narrower at the bottom. Notice how the top gets thicker. Simplify the details by drawing only one knob on each drawer.

MORE chibi pROps

The sky's the limit when it comes to chibi props. Fantasy warrior characters may need swords, magical staffs, armor, and shields. A chibi athlete could use baseballs, hockey sticks, or tennis racquets. Then there are everyday objects like flowers, brooms, and video game controllers. Take a look at a few random props below.

SWORD
The chibi sword's blade is pointed, and the hilt and handle are short. The handle gets fatter toward the end, rather than staying the same width.

BROOM
The chibi broom is shorter and fatter than a normal broom. Its broomstick is slightly uneven, and the straw has rounded edges.

MAGICAL STAFF
Any fantasy buff is familiar with magical staffs and wands. Our design is fairly common: It has a long wooden base with a gnarled top, and holds a gemstone.

FLOWER
The chibi daisy has five petals, the flower's center is a smooth circle, and the stem is shorter and wider. When drawing other detail-rich flowers, like roses, in chibi style, exaggerate key features that capture the essence of the flower.

putting it all together

Now it's time to apply everything you've learned to draw a chibi scene. Start with basic shapes to plan your drawing. Then add one thing at a time. Some artists start with characters; others start with objects. Take your time and experiment to see what works for you.

STEP ONE Start with basic shapes and guidelines. Know what kind of composition you want for your drawing before you begin.

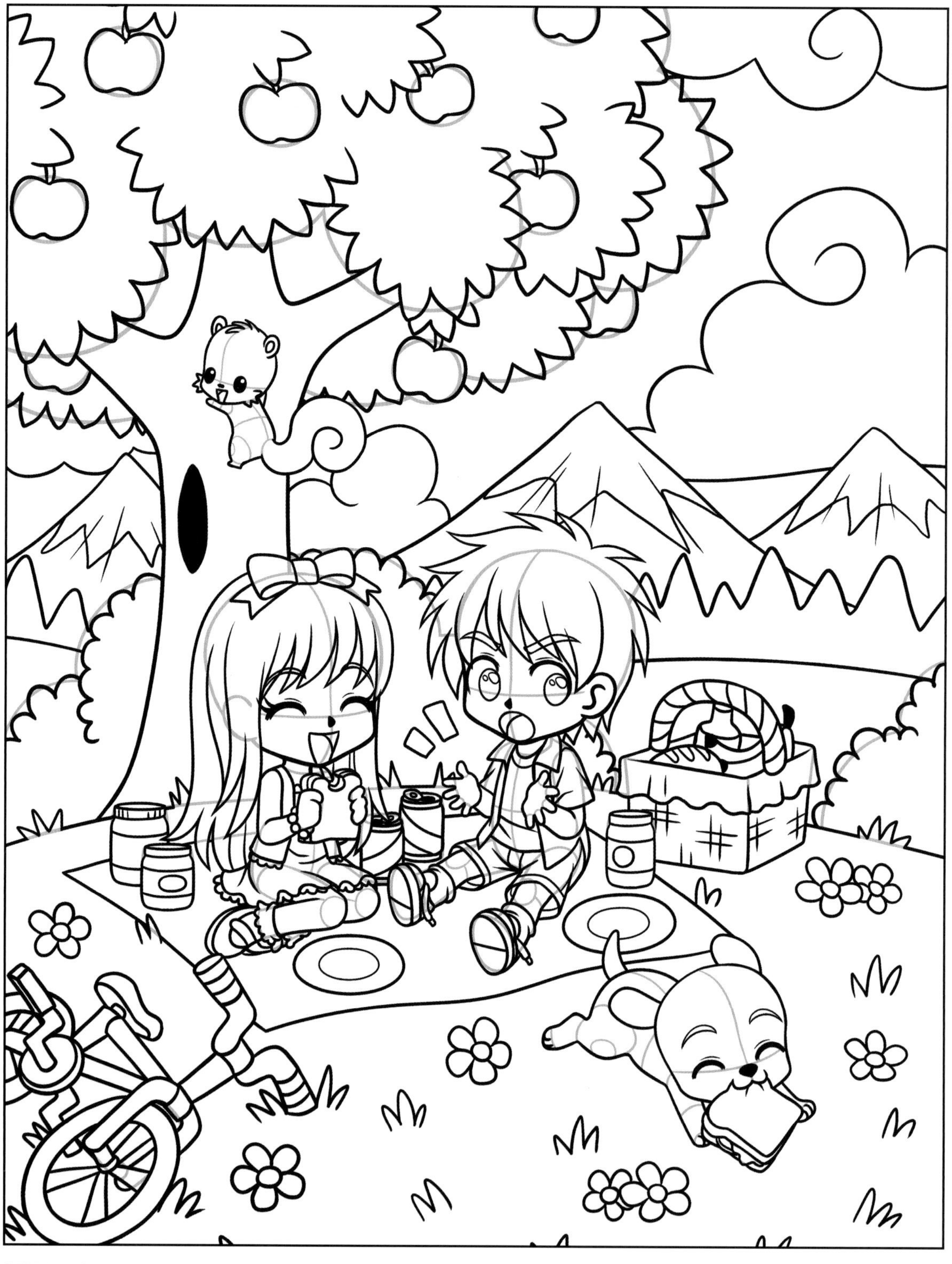

STEP TWO In this step, draw in your details. Decide what the characters are wearing and holding, and what kind of expressions they have. After you finish the characters, tackle other details.

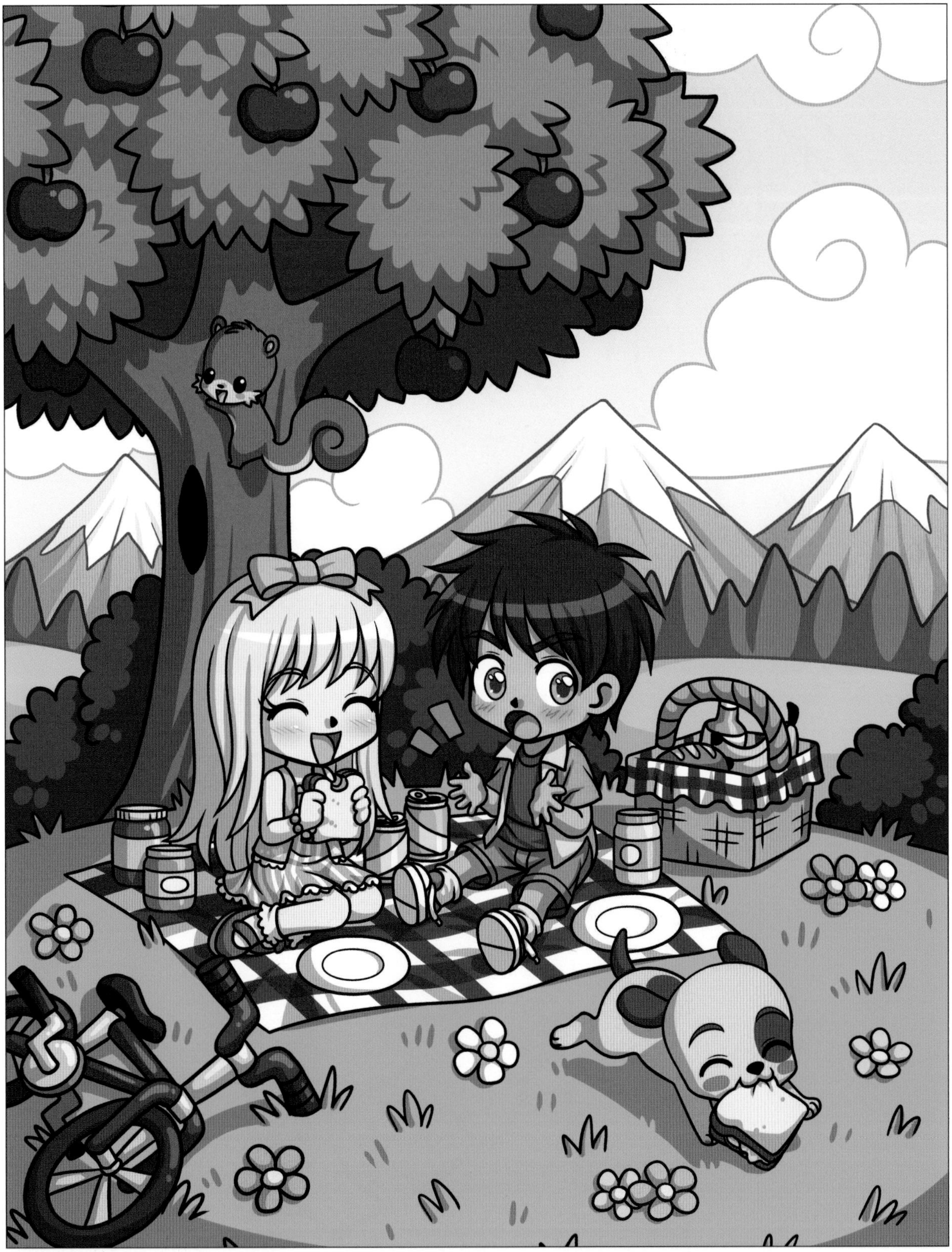

STEP THREE Start by choosing your light source, which will define the placement of shadows. Also think about what time of day it is because it affects how you'll color your illustration. Objects that are farther away should be more faded and less detailed. The main subject(s) of your drawing should have clearly defined details so that they are the focal point.

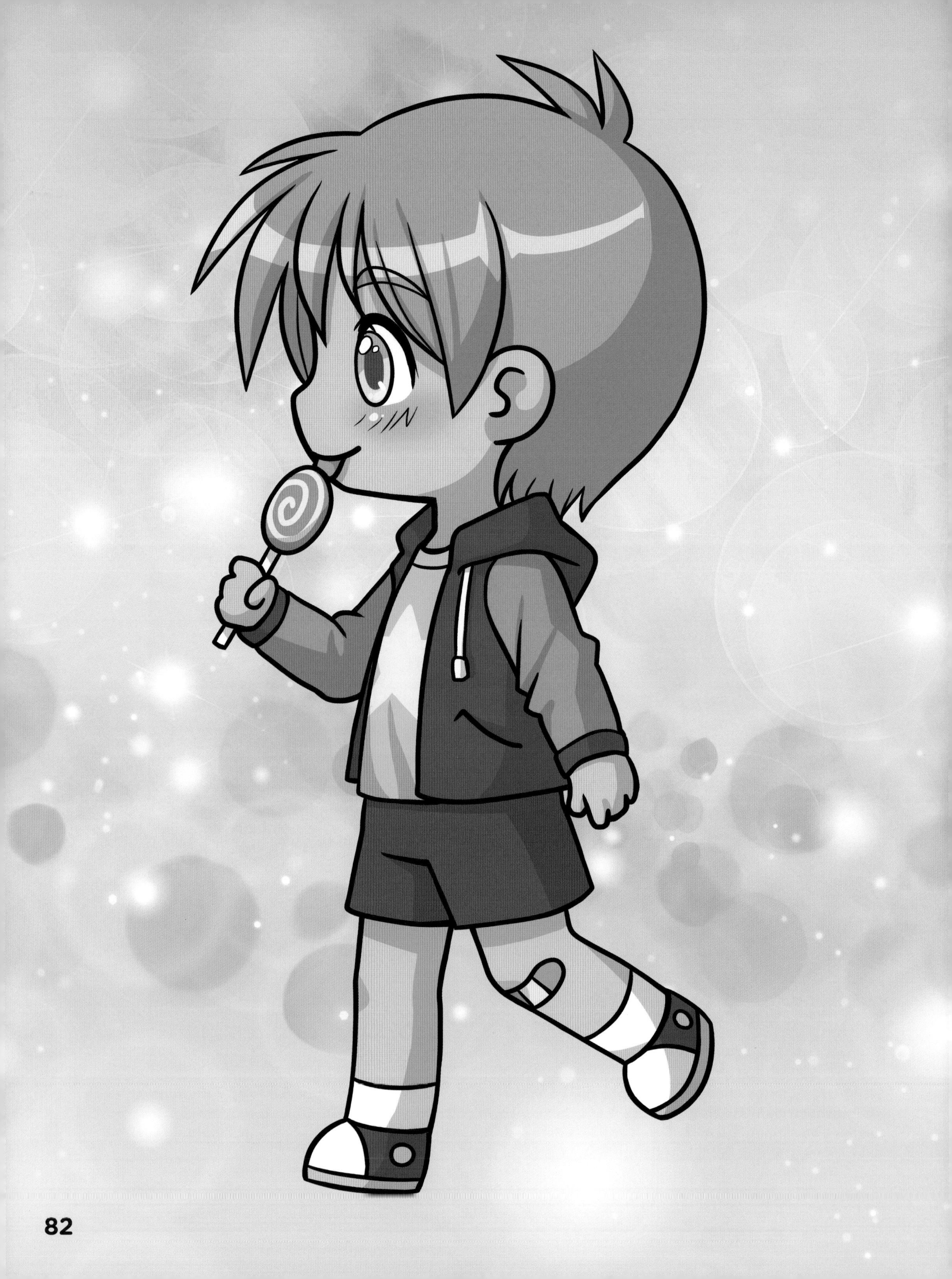

chapter 5

templates

chibi expressions

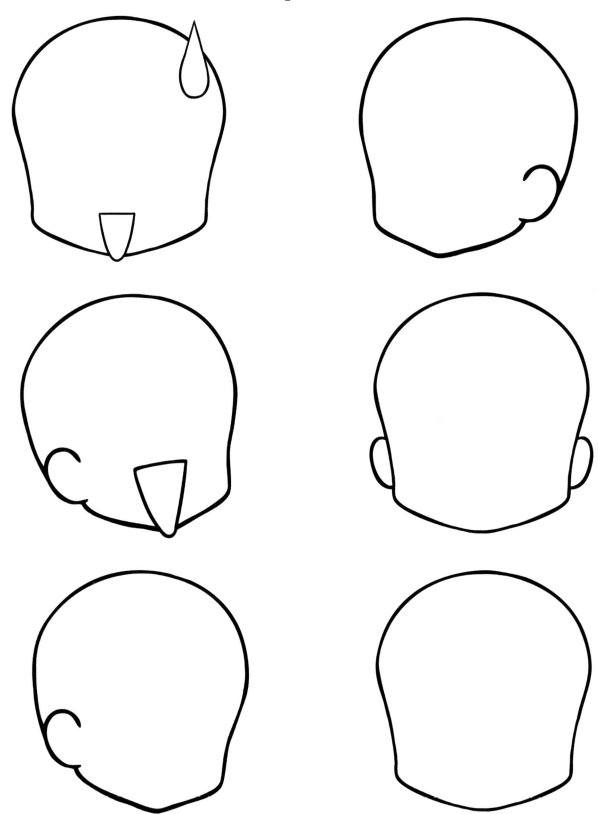

chibi ³/₄ view

jumping

excited

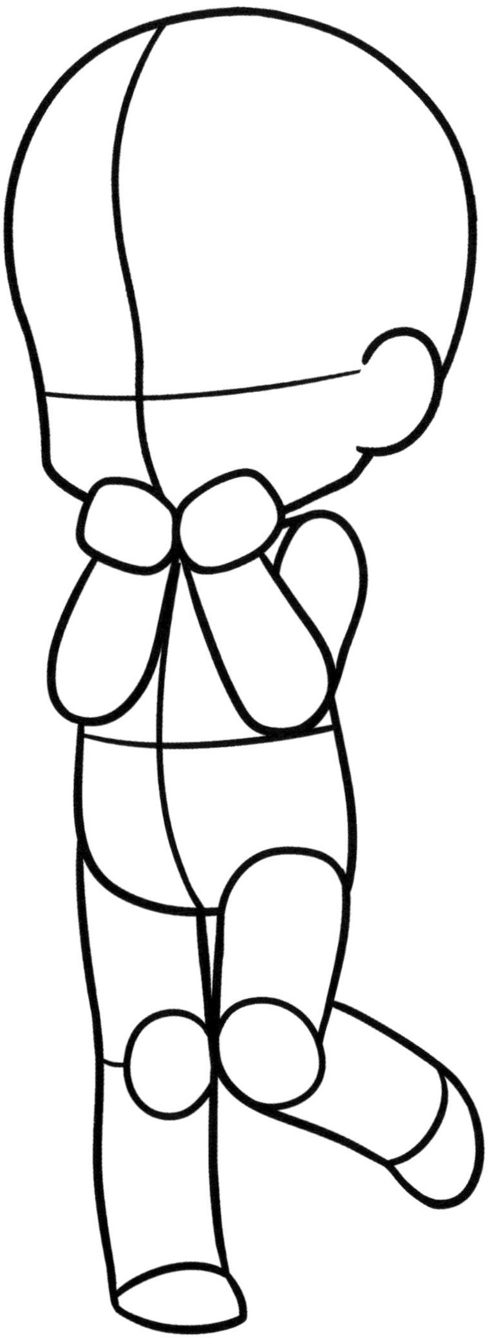

victory

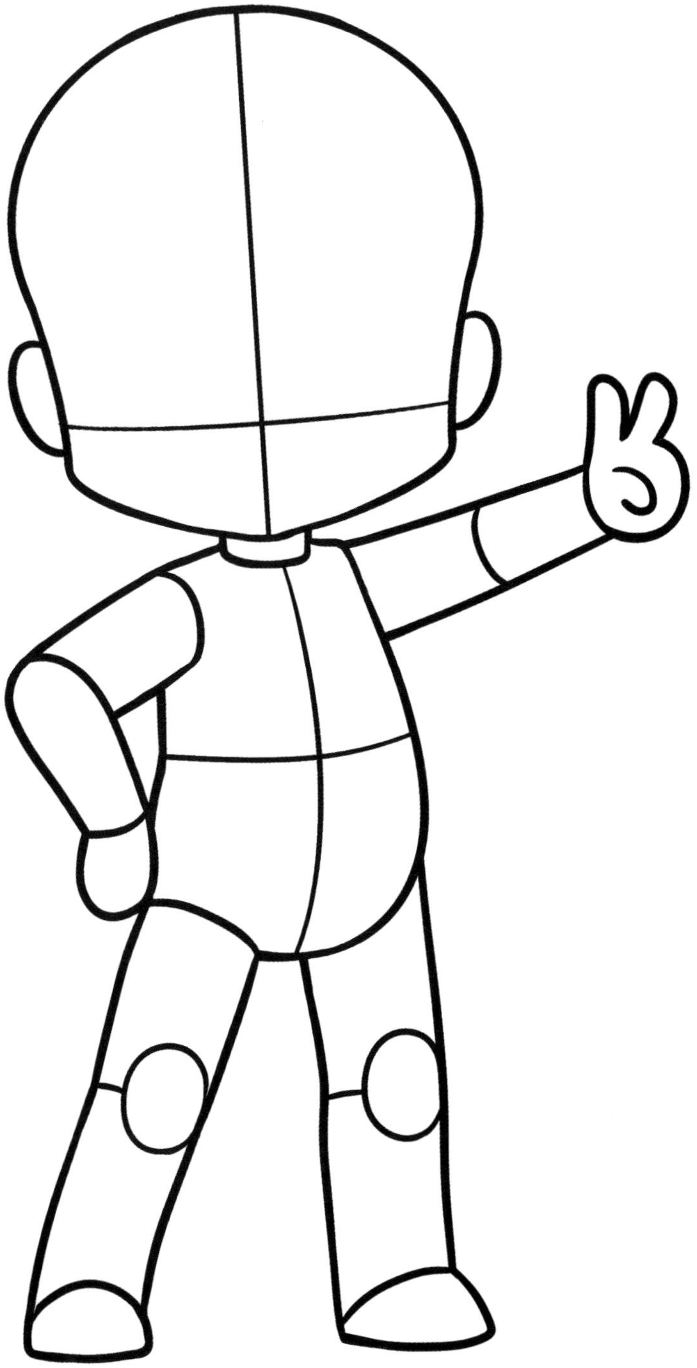

superhero

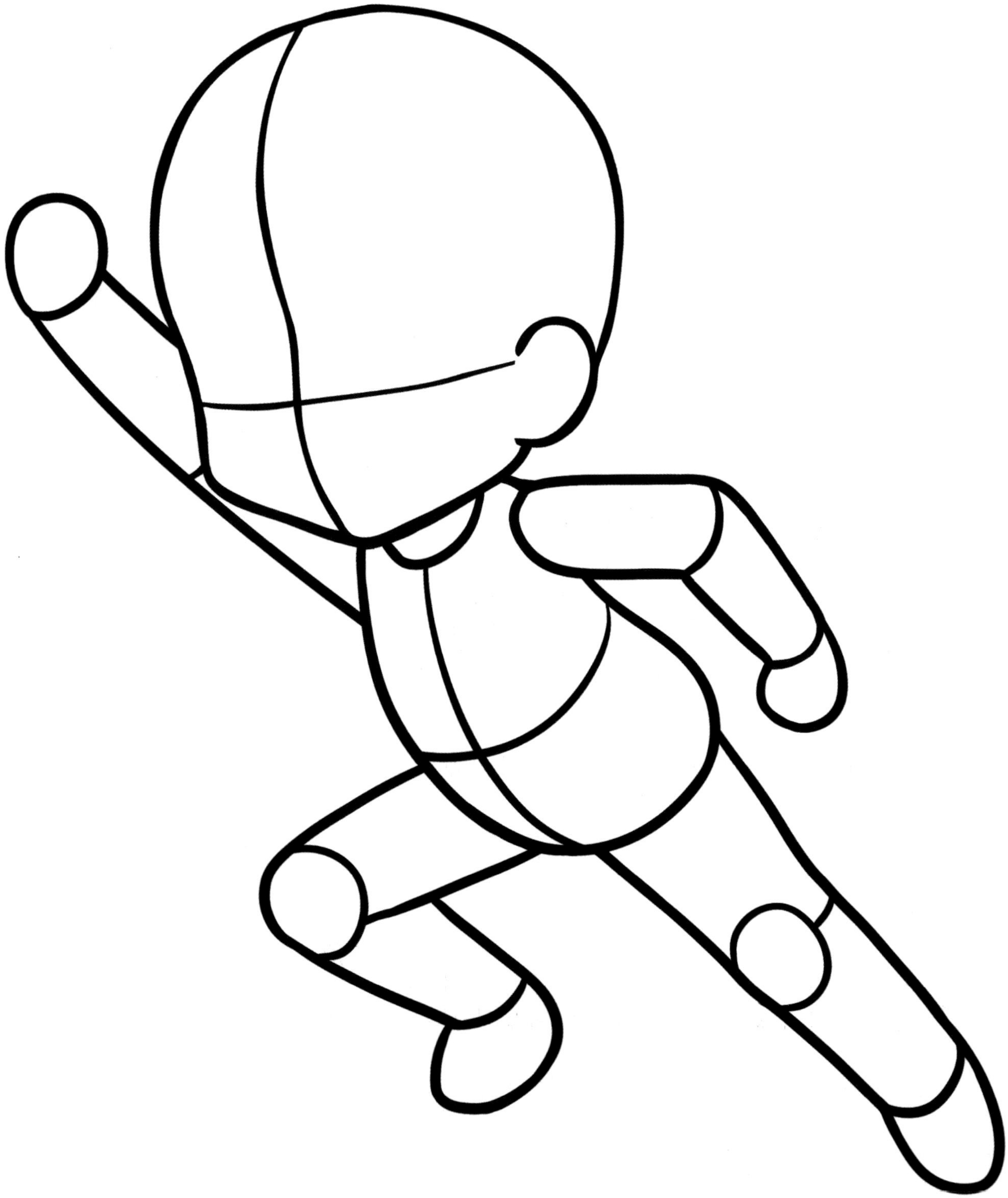

fLying

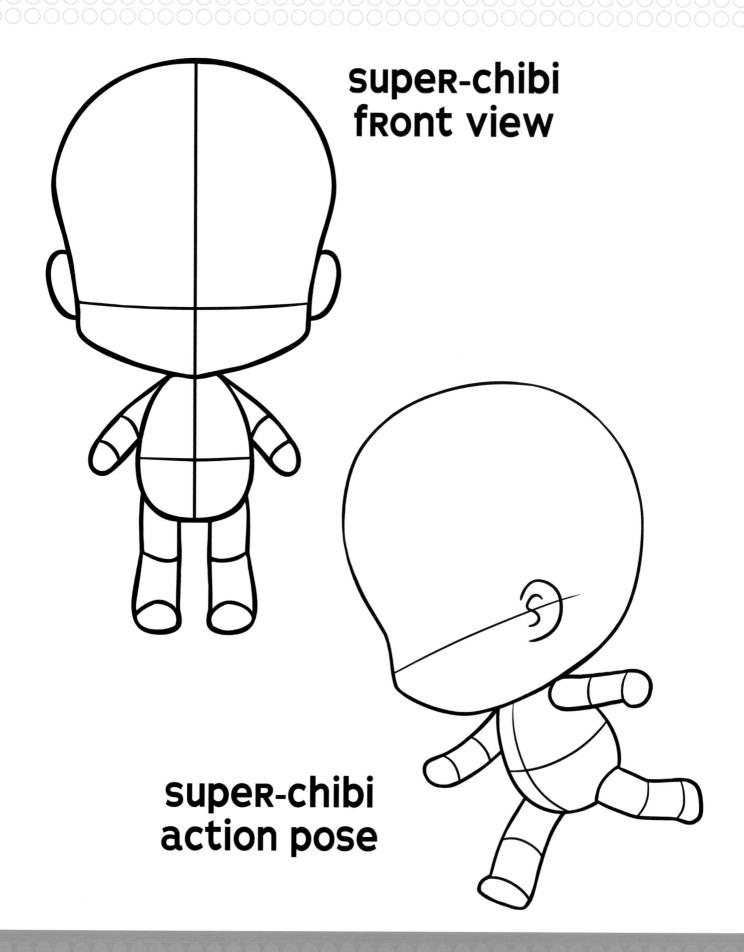

super-chibi
front view

super-chibi
action pose

two-legged critter front view

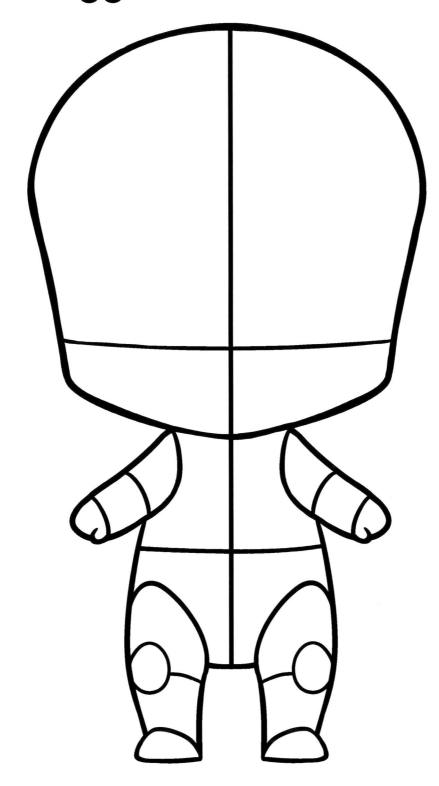

four-Legged critter side view

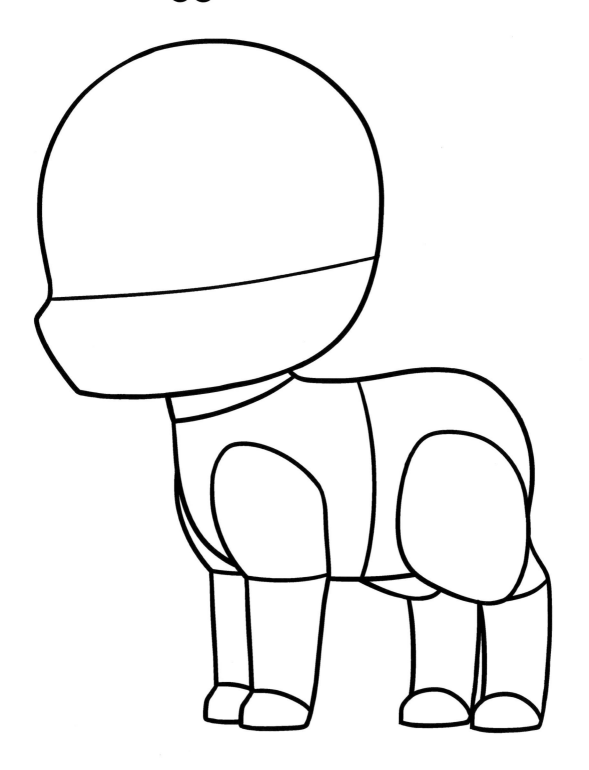

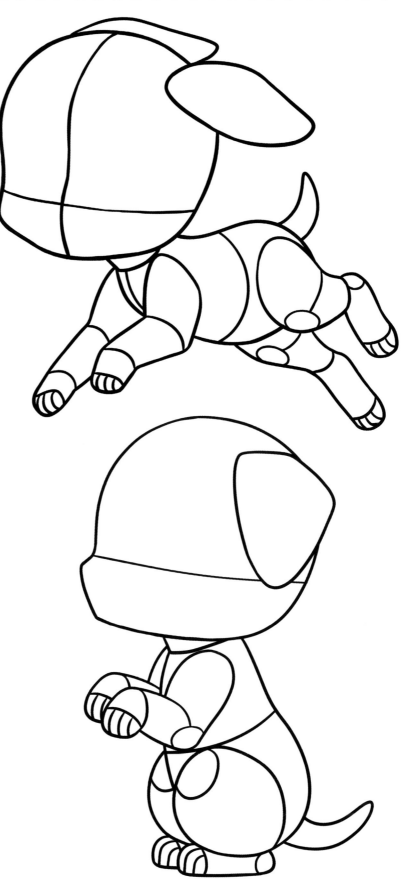

**dog
running**

**dog
begging**

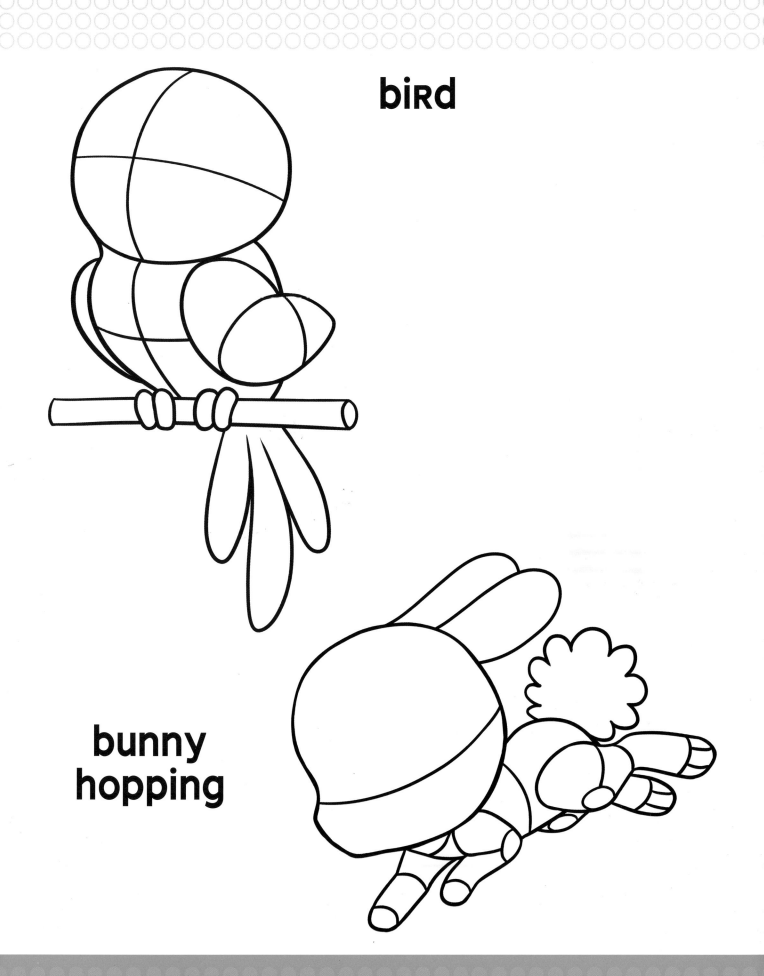

bird

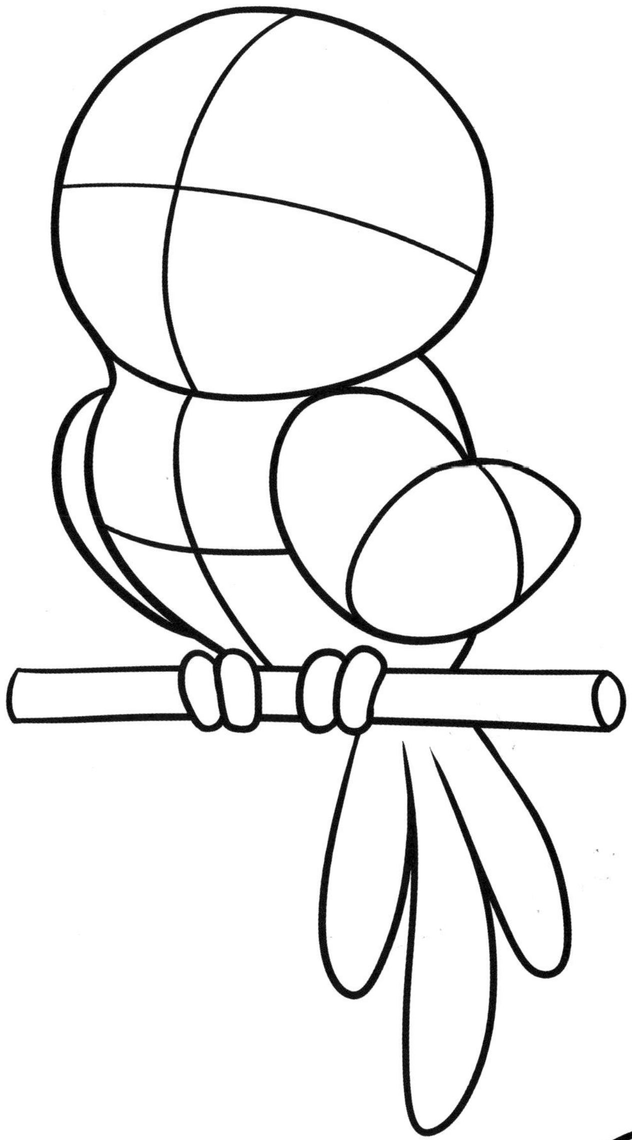

bunny hopping

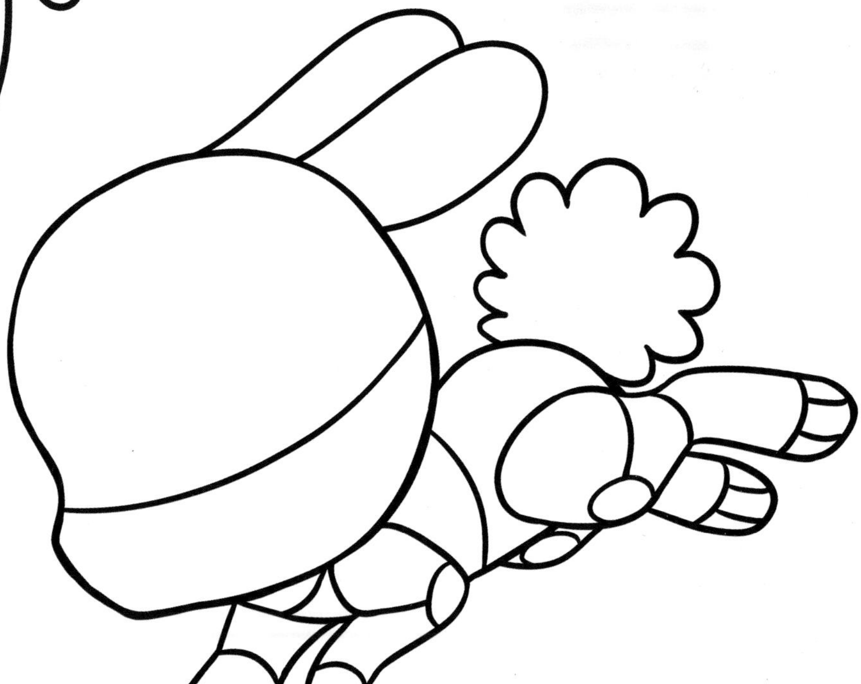

about the artists

Samantha Whitten is a full-time freelance artist who specializes in creating art of adorable! She has spent all of her life drawing and has pursued a career in illustration and graphic design, learning on her own and dabbling in a variety of projects. These days she earns a living by selling a unique range of products featuring her artwork, employing a cute and fun style that appeals to all ages, as well as illustrating various web comics in her spare time. Visit www.littlecelesse.com.

Jeannie Lee's art education includes more than seven years of instruction under contemporary Western artist Ji Young Oh, as well as two years studying traditional character animation at California Institute of the Arts. Jeannine has worked for Gaia Interactive, Marvel Entertainment, Inc., TOKYOPOP, and UDON Entertainment.

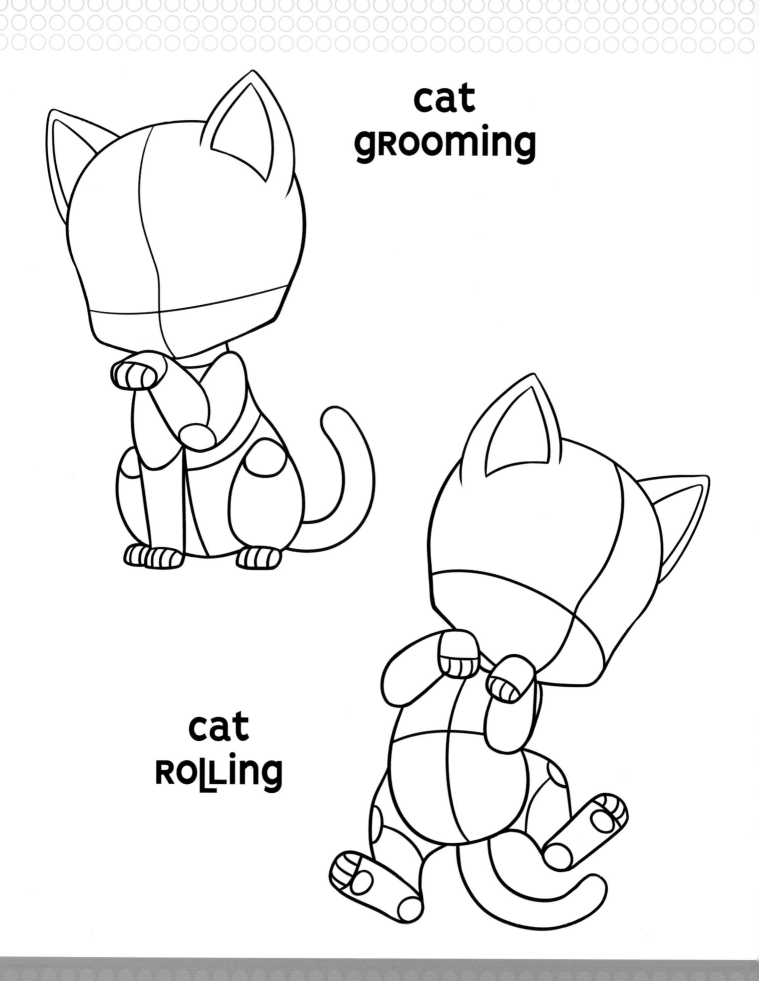

cat grooming

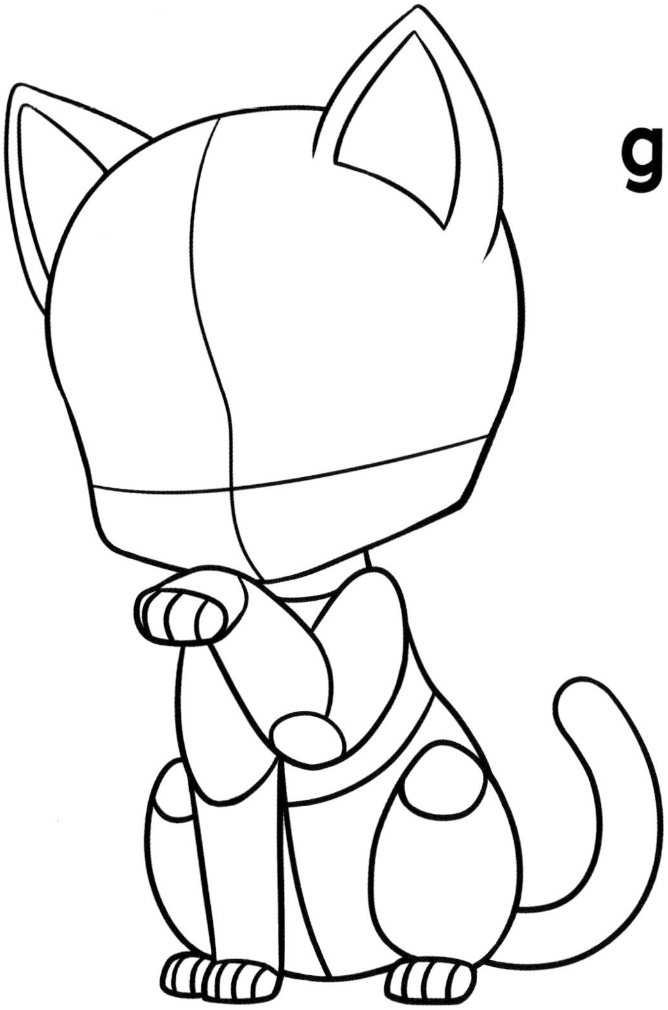

cat rolling

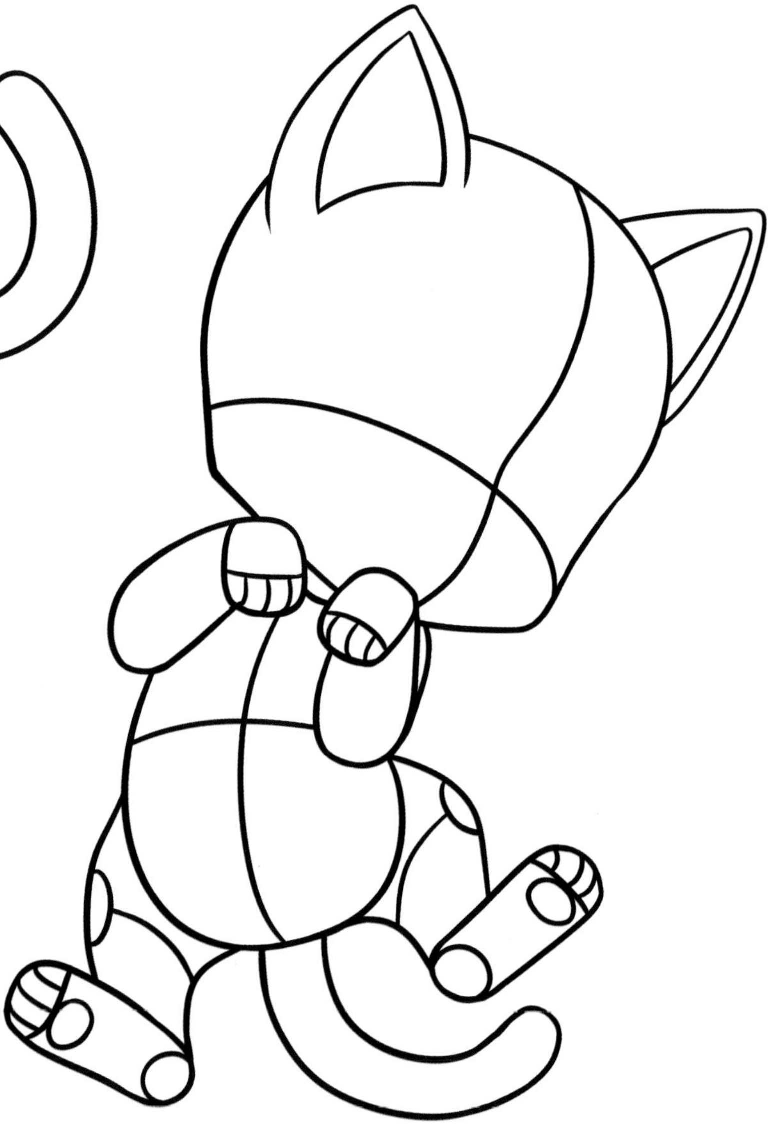